Famous Artists Annual 1

FAMOUS ARTISTS ANNUAL 1

A Treasury of Contemporary Art

FAMOUS ARTISTS SCHOOLS, INC.
Westport, Connecticut

Staff for this book

Editor: Milton Rugoff
Associate Editor: Constance Sullivan
Art Director: Ulrich Ruchti
Assistant Art Director: Ellen Hsiao
Picture Consultants: Shareen Blair and
Gerald McConnell
Production: Gudrun Buettner
Advisors for Famous Artists School:
Fred Ludekens and Austin Briggs
Planned and produced
under the supervision of Chanticleer Press,
Paul Steiner, Publisher

This book is set in Helvetica
and printed in
monochrome and color gravure by
Conzett & Huber, Zurich, Switzerland

All rights reserved under
International and Pan-American Copyright Conventions.
Published by the Famous Artists Schools,
Westport, Connecticut.
SBN 8038–2267–7
Library of Congress Catalog Number: 78–97767

Contents

The purpose of this book

The purpose of this book is to open up to you the whole exciting world of art by presenting what is being done in every major field—painting, graphics, sculpture, illustration, advertising, theater design, and so forth—including by whom, for whom, how and why.

Whether your chief interest is fine or commercial art, you will find in the following pages examples of the best contemporary work of that kind. In the text various authorities illuminate these subjects with an informative commentary, while some of the artists themselves share with us their ideas, theories and methods in their own words.

It is in the nature of many artists today to take an expansive interest in the human situation and environment. Few of us can any longer afford to be isolated, either from humanity in general or from our colleagues. The popular magazine illustrator and advertising artist is as likely to be influenced by the latest exhibition at a museum of modern art as avant-garde painters and sculptors may be influenced by what is happening in advertising, fashion, or industrial design. Essential to a mature knowledge and understanding is a degree of familiarity with all the arts.

You will find in the trends, currents, and cross currents presented in this volume a treasury of inspiration and ideas. It is quite possible, too, that you will be surprised, puzzled, or even repelled by some of what you see. This is only to be expected in such an all-inclusive anthology. In viewing and evaluating creative work the point is not merely to like or not to like—or even, for that matter, immediately and completely to understand. It is to experience, to feel, and through experience and feeling eventually to know. Accomplishing this depends on a confrontation with the new and unfamiliar as well as a continued enjoyment of the comfortably sound and traditional.

You would have to visit dozens of galleries and museums, talk to many of the best-known artists, read the most recent illustrated magazines to see and experience what this volume puts at your disposal. That, however, need not be the end of the matter. It is our intention, and sincere hope, that the Annual allows room for exploration and growth—your growth into a broader, deeper, and ever more enjoyable knowledge of art.

FRED LUDEKENS

1 Background

The Role of the Artist

by Charlotte Willard

The artist has always been a special breed of man. Looking for answers, asking questions, he has never been content to let things be. What Picasso calls "the sun in my belly" has always compelled him to invent, to create something out of nothing. To make magic. Wood, stone, clay, metal, charcoal, paint became, under his hand, the whole world. The heavens and hell, gods and goddesses, the seven seas, the beasts in the field and the birds in the air, all mankind, the artist created again and again. He has even made the invisible visible, giving visual form to what man has thought, what he has felt. It is no wonder then that artists for centuries have been the priests, teachers, explorers, experimenters, magicians.

The artist-priest among primitive people was a potent instrument for survival. As doctor who cured all ills with his masks and incantation, his fetishes and magic objects, he was charged with averting disasters and attracting good luck. As master of tribal ceremonies, he gave his followers the consolations of community rituals, and the bonds of common beliefs. He was, in fact, the earliest insurance agent—one who could protect man against the uncertainties of life and help him face the finalities of death. The prehistoric artists who painted on the walls of Lascaux and Dordogne were probably such artist-priests. Their brilliantly painted friezes of bison and deer were perhaps created to insure good hunting by identifying the prey. The artist's tasks were to create objects that could readily be identified, which would, at the same time, be symbols that conveyed to man the wonders and mysteries of the universe. Every artist, then, in Africa, Mexico, India, China, and Alaska, had to become familiar with the outward forms of their subjects—man, trees, animals, birds, fishes. This compelled them to be keen observers, turning them, so to speak, into the first scientists.

The Coatlique, the Aztec Goddess of Death, with its necklaces of serpents and its belt of skulls, its death's-head as a face, is probably the most condensed form of terror ever invented by man. The great masks and figures of Africa,

the Kuan Yin of China whose benign presence radiates serenity across the centuries, the shaman masks of Northwest America, of Japan and New Guinea, are examples of the work of artist-priests who used art in their functions as protectors, teachers, prophets, with visible power.

The primitive sculptors of Egypt who constructed giant monuments to the monolithic power of their civilization, condensed the history of dynasties and created enduring revelations of the state of man. The Great Sphinx, half human, half beast, is still a potent symbol of the human condition.

Early Greek sculptors were the first to create gods in man's image. Their goddess of love, Aphrodite, is still the synonym for beauty, and the Apollo is the western world's masculine ideal. Unlike the Egyptians, whose culture centered around death and the hereafter, the Greeks celebrated life, here and now. They worshipped love, wisdom, courage, exalted the human body. Their artists dealt with man's great triumphs, his intelligence, his strength and his beauty. They invented heroes, God-men, free to think and act without threats of dire punishments in afterlife. Artists gave the Greeks a vision of themselves that helped them achieve ideals that are in great measure the foundations of Western culture.

During the Middle Ages, when Christianity was the faith and refuge of millions, the artist, anonymous and humble, poured his religious feelings into his art. Few symbols of that mystical holiness which we ascribe to the divine can equal the Christ and the Virgin in the Cathedral of Chartres. Carved in stone and immortalized in stained glass, the figures at Chartres attain an emotional life rarely matched in art. While the Christian Church established a priesthood to propagate the faith, the Church turned to artists for ways to reach the masses of people. It is difficult to imagine Christianity without the Madonnas of Cimabue, Fra Angelico or Giotto, without the great biblical characters of Piero Della Francesca, or Michelangelo's "Last

Judgment" in the Sistine Chapel. In the heyday of the Renaissance, emperors and Popes vied with each other to enlist the greatest artists for their projects. Popes Julius II and Paul III fought the Medici for the services of Michelangelo. Charles V, emperor of the Holy Roman Empire, was happy to hold the brushes of Titian while the artist painted his portrait.

Yet even while working for the Church, artists played another role—that of explorer of science, experimenter and teacher. Leonardo da Vinci is the prime example of this. A "Renaissance Man," he was, as we know, not only a master of anatomy, but of optics, aerodynamics, mechanics, botany, geology, archeology.

He was not alone. Van Eyck discovered that oils mixed with pigment were longer lasting than the egg tempera then in current use. Uccello, who could make space with color, was also devoted to mathematics. This discipline led him to the science of perspective. Dürer worked on mathematical proportions of the human figure. Caravaggio discovered that light could focus maximum attention on his central figures. Rembrandt refined these ideas and carried the treatment of light to new boundaries, creating illuminations of divinity that earlier artists could only suggest with the halo. Going further than any artist before him, he said that God created man in his own image—all men, so that he painted his street beggars and Jews as if they were kings and taught us that all men are brothers.

From the Renaissance, when they were propagandists for the Church and the kings, to our time, when artists must seek private patrons but are free to choose the field of their interests, the role of the artist has changed. He has been largely relegated to the outskirts of society. Yet today one can perceive a prevailing direction. It is one that is increasingly tied to modern science and technology. More than ever in the last two hundred years the goal of many great artists has moved parallel to the endless search of scientists for the reality behind appearances. Perhaps in the work of Goya we can find the

bridge between the art of the Renaissance and modern painting. His "Black" paintings, his "Caprichos," predate Freud's exploration of the unconscious and gave shape to the grim terrors that overshadow our psyche. It was Turner, however, with paintings that are visual expositions on the relationship between color and light and their effect on material objects, who pioneered in this field. Precursor of the Impressionists, and ancestor to Seurat, he arrived intuitively at the concept that light is a form of primal energy, and color is one manifestation of light.

With Cézanne, art moved into the realm of abstraction, not because he painted abstract pictures, but because he employed geometric principles in creating them. He reduced all forms in nature to the sphere, the cylinder, and the cone. Suggesting the near and the far by color alone, he discarded classical perspective, and based his still lifes, landscapes and portraits on the movement and countermovement, the compression and expansion, that are basic forces in the universe.

The Cubists, such as Picasso, Braque, Juan Gris, and Naum Gabo, carried the theories of abstract form further when they interpreted the world in geometric formulations. Gabo's famous "Cubist Madonna" shows how such scientific ideas could be transformed by the magic of art to produce evocative and magnetic images. An art movement in himself, Picasso had demonstrated that a static painting or sculpture could, without mechanical motion, show more than one aspect of a face or a figure—the front and profile, the figure still and in action. A magician who can transform a toy automobile into the head of a baboon, who can use color to suggest joy or sorrow, the fragrance of flowers, the taste of tropical fruit, Picasso is the greatest shaman of the twentieth century.

Other artists of the twentieth century have opened many new paths for painting and sculpture. Art, they proclaimed, must have no shackles. The Fauves liberated color from nature so that a horse could be purple and a woman's face green and orange. This was color as it was

used by the primitive artist-priests . . . color not imitating nature but chosen to invoke the feelings of joy or terror.

The Constructivists declared art must be free of subject matter. Malevich, with his "Black Square on White" and his famous "White on White" painting, probably sounded the first clear note in this abstract direction. Kandinsky declared that painting needed no other subject matter than itself. First to paint abstract expressionist canvases that are a blazing turbulence of color in motion, Kandinsky was greatly influenced by Einstein's theory that matter is composed of invisible atoms in constant motion. Mondrian proposed that colors have weight and expansive qualities that could be calculated to reflect the balance and harmony in the invisible world. His immaculate squares of primary colors are lyrical demonstrations of his theories.

The machine early in the century also began to figure in the paintings and sculptures of the modern artist. Welcomed, hated and feared, loved and revered, the machine is still a contemporary obsession. Léger was the first to devote his life to interpreting the world in terms of the machine. He believed it might lighten the work of man. De Chirico was not so optimistic. His faceless mannequins are prophecies of the thoughtless, detached contemporary man which the machine has too often produced. Trova issues further dire prophecies. His "Man" is armless, impotent, falling, too often an appendage to the machine that uses him like a replaceable part. For Tinguely, the machine is a monster that will ultimately destroy itself. His "Homage to New York" did just that.

Following Freud, the Surrealist movement probed the rich world of the unconscious, inhabited by our loves and our hates, our fears and our joys. The work of Ernst, Dali, Magritte, bring to the surface our contemporary anxieties in their irrational but vivid paintings and sculptures just as the witch doctors' totems and masks gave shape to the terrors and aspirations of the primitive world. Among the many other movements afoot, perhaps the most

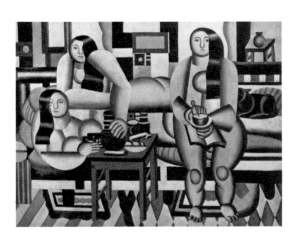

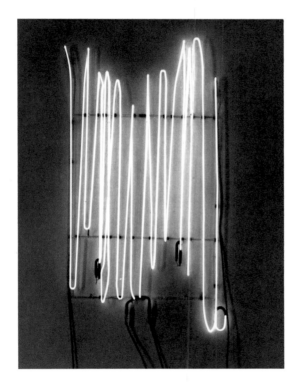

pervasive direction discernible today is the dematerialization of art.

Op art, kinetic art, "Light" art are aspects of this trend. Op art by retinal irritation produces images that are not present, colors that are not painted, forms that shift and change. The works of Anuszkiewicz, Larry Poons, Bridget Riley and Victor Vasarely are examples of this practice, and Israeli painter Agam depends on structural devices to transform his works as you move about them. Such pieces graphically illustrate the modern theory that nothing is static, that art must mirror the flow of life whose only certain characteristic is change.

Kinetic art has many manifestations. Motors, gravity or wind—as in mobiles—are used to obtain motion. Len Lye carries the dematerialization of art to the point where his motorized sculptures disappear as material objects, leaving only an ethereal vision of movement in space for pure contemplation. In "Light" art, dematerialization reaches its almost total realization. Light is used to make shapes and colors formerly created by paint. Using programmed circuits, slide projections, reflections, artists are transforming the art of the object into art that is in process or becoming. Light objects such as fluorescent tubes or the light cast on a wall hold the art experience, not the object itself. Several artists also produce work that is constructed to change by programmed patternings or by the action of the viewer. The art becomes a responsive relationship between the machine and the artist and the viewer.

What does all this mean and where will it end? These trends will not only change the nature of art but may well transform the world. All clues point to an art that will no longer be found in museums or on the walls of homes. Art will influence our total environment. It will be a public art that will change our streets and buildings, and enrich our cities and our roads with color and light. It will be an art for all the people, open to all, to be enjoyed by everyone. Should this happen, the artist-magician will again assume a major role in our society.

2 New Work

In the Sixties

by Elenore Lester

American art of the 1960's represented a radical turning away from the Abstract Expressionism that had dominated art in the preceding decade. Abstract Expressionism, also called Action painting, was a highly subjective movement. The Abstract Expressionist's work was a kind of psychic biography, a record of the artist's accumulated experience and creative living at the moment of making the picture. During the 1960's, young artists searching for new horizons turned away from this intense subjectivity and reached toward the objective world.

The change did not come overnight. There were many prophetic signs in the Fifties. In 1953 one of the controversial events in art was a show in which Larry Rivers, a young painter out of the Abstract Expressionist school, introduced identifiable images into his canvases. His "Washington Crossing the Delaware," showing the blurred faces and figures of revolutionary heroes, had some critics wondering whether there was to be a return to old-fashioned naturalism. In the same year, another young Abstract Expressionist, Robert Rauschenberg, created a mixed-media work, "The Bed," which was quite simply a bed made of paint and fabric on canvas. Five years later, another young painter, Jasper Johns, introduced in his first one-man show in New York a series of enigmatic canvases made up of isolated images out of everyday life painted with meticulous care—the American flag, a target, numbers or letters running up and down the picture. In some cases, actual objects were stuck into the canvas—a shelf of boxes containing plaster casts of anatomical parts, a wooden drawer, a wire coat-hanger. And in the same year, Allan Kaprow, paying tribute to Abstract Expressionist Jackson Pollock, said that Action painting "left us at a point where we must become preoccupied and even dazzled by the space and objects of our everyday life . . . objects of every sort are the material for the new art: paint, chairs, food, electric and neon lights, smoke, water, old socks, a dog, movies, a thousand other things which will be discovered by the present generation of artists."

Those who saw in these signs a return to the realism of the past were wrong. The young artists had drawn deep inspiration from Pollock, Mark Rothko, Barnett Newman and Willem deKooning, and they were digging back to the original sources of Abstract Expressionism—Dada, Surrealism and various "pure" forms of abstractionism. Unlike the realism of the past, which is based on the concept that the canvas is a kind of window through which the artist points out his conception of the world, the work of the new American realists was designed to provide the viewer with a head-on collision with some aspect of actuality.

This is true of four separate categories of art in the Sixties—Pop, Op, minimal and environmental or intermedia. Each in very different ways stripped the art viewer of esthetic preconceptions and jolted him into a heightened awareness of his own responses. He could not stand back and admire the artist's virtuoso skill in composition, brushwork, draughtsmanship, or even in Abstract Expressionism, the artist's ability to realize, in non-imagistic terms, his inner being. The art of the Sixties lacked these qualities and the viewer was left wondering: What is art? What is the difference between art and life? Rauschenberg's statement "Painting relates to both art and life. Neither can be made. (I try to act in that gap between the two.)" was quoted throughout the decade.

Jackson Pollock (top)
No. 8, 1949.
Collection of Mr. and Mrs. Roy R. Neuberger.
(Museum of Modern Art, New York)

Barnet Newman (bottom)
Triad, 1965.
Collection John and Kimiko Powers.

Brillo boxes and soup cans

The use by Rivers, Rauschenberg and Johns of commonplace images and objects as an art product helped prepare the way for Pop artists Andy Warhol, Tom Wesselman, Jim Rosenquist, Claes Oldenburg and Jim Dine. Whereas Rivers, Rauschenberg and Johns selected certain objects to make a cryptic art statement, the Pop artists raided the full range of visual possibilities offered by our technologized environment. They zestfully employed the latest plastics and reproduction devices in their work. Interestingly enough, most of the Pop artists had worked in commercial art and were saturated with a feeling for the principles and visual sensibilities in advertising. Warhol had been a top New York fashion illustrator for a decade. Lichtenstein had worked on comic strips and Rosenquist had been a billboard artist. They utilized images and techniques fa-

miliar to them and the general public—not merely to art gallery goers. A large new public was delighted by Warhol's Brillo boxes and Campbell soup cans exhibited as art. Similarly, Oldenburg's soft sculptures (made of fabric or vinyl) of clothing and typewriters and his plaster-and-paint hamburgers, Lichtenstein's blown-up comic-strip panels, Wesselman's plastic bathroom collages and Rosenquist's billboard segments, all gave the art public the unsettling yet titillating experience of being confronted with images out of their culture, isolated and presented as art.

In contrast to realists who said to the art viewer, "I will show you the beauty I see in this landscape (or person)," the Pop artist said simply, "Here is what you see every day. Make of it what you can." Warhol and Lichtenstein particularly emphasized the mechanical aspect of the everyday visual world. By silk-screening newspaper photos of two contemporary goddesses—Marilyn Monroe and Jackie Kennedy—and running the pictures in a series, Warhol stressed their intrinsic nature as "images," at once potent and soporific. Lichtenstein similarly reported coolly on the brash, vital, comic-strip world by using a projector to enlarge his subjects. To emphasize the look of the newspaper picture, he even put in the tiny dots that are the marks of the newspicture reproduction process. Oldenburg brought a more personal sensibility to his images of food and clothing. His almost obscene pies, sundaes, hamburgers suggested the relationship between digestion and excretion, and his gigantic limp "sculptures" of clothing and such commonplace objects as light switches, suggested the walking dream of everyday life in which we wander helplessly among the objects that make up our existence and to which we have no dynamic relation.

Although the kinship between Pop and Dada was often noted, it should be remembered that Dada was a passionate protest against the society that had given rise to the mechanized barbarism of World War I. In contrast, the Pop artists were cool, wry, and seemed to be sharing an "in" joke with the art audience. Far from wanting to destroy the culture, the Pop artists revealed a robust delight in the garishness of the scene, and far from being outraged, as were the stolid European bourgeoisie by Dada, American art consumers took the Pop artists to their hearts. The Establishment showered these artists with money, prizes and academic honors.

Jasper Johns
Painted Bronze, 1964.
(Leo Castelli Gallery)

Ellsworth Kelly (top)
2 Panels: Blue Red, 1968.
(Sidney Janis Gallery)

Frank Stella (above)
Tahki-I-Sulayman I, 1967.
Collection Robert Rowan.
(Leo Castelli Gallery)

The minimal approach

From a very different European source, another group of American artists of the Sixties took an entirely different approach to reality. During World War I, shortly after the Dadaists became active, two Russian artists, Naum Gabo and Kasimir Malevich, declared that the subject of a work of art is the art image itself; it should not represent anything or even suggest anything. There was to be no chiaroscuro or shading that might suggest volume, space, mood or illusion, and the image was not to depend on any "automatic" gesture or any emanation from the unconscious. The painting was to look like paint on canvas, untouched by human hands. This, of course, differed totally from the Abstract Expressionist ideal that the art image was created out of inner necessity. The Dutch painter of carefully composed rectangles in black, white and primary colors, Piet Mondriaan, and the German Joseph Albers, who juxtaposed geometric forms, both of whom came to the United States with Dadaist and Surrealist painters in World War II, helped to disseminate versions of Constructivist theory.

Constructivism went underground when Abstract Expressionism took over the art scene, but in the Sixties it re-emerged in the form of hard-edge, minimal or "color field" painting. Ellsworth Kelly's checkerboard squares and broad rectangles of color, Frank Stella's meticulously painted chevrons and Robert Louis's heraldic stripes all proclaimed the doctrine that a painting is a painting is a painting. For these artists "the real" meant the actual physical fact of shape and color on canvas. In order to get away from any lingering suggestion of illusionism they soaked color directly into raw canvas, often using acrylic paints for a texture that seemed to unite paint and canvas more closely. There was one step further to go—destroy the rectangular frame which suggested that something was being translated onto the canvas. Stella and Kelly cut and shaped their canvases to conform with the painted design. Thus the image was at last entirely one with the canvas. The minimalists, according to critic E. C. Goosen, were really close in aim to such Abstract Expressionists as Pollock, Rothko, Newman and Clyfford Still. They were out to "find one's real self on the canvas through personal imagery and format."

Robert Morris
Untitled, 1965, galvanized iron.
(Leo Castelli Gallery)

Robert Smithson
Plunge, 1966, painted steel.
(Dwan Gallery)

Minimal sculpture

Allied to minimal painting was minimal sculpture, perhaps the only "pure" sculpture of the Sixties. It emphasized the physical actuality of the work of art. "Sculpture is what I bump into when I step back to look at a painting," said Ad Reinhardt, who was a minimal painter without the label throughout the years of Abstract Expressionism. His comment captured the essence of a movement which challenged the concept that sculpture must carve or enclose space. Large clean, solid chunks of metals, wood or synthetics were placed on the floor, hung from the ceiling, attached to walls or leaned against walls. Plinths or pedestals were eliminated. The object was what it was, nothing more—a slab of perforated steel or eight galvanized iron rectangular boxes attached to the walls (Don Judd), four aluminum beams forming a square and propped up at one end by two aluminum supports (Robert Morris), a rectangular slab of hard blue plastic propped up against a wall (John McCracken), a six-foot steel cube (Tony Smith). There was much interest in surface quality, with some sculptors using paint or the very bright colors of synthetics, and others utilizing the straightforward industrial gray of metals. Perhaps the most disconcerting aspect of this sculpture was that a good many of the artists boasted of never having touched the work with their own hands. They had simply ordered it cut to specifications from supply shops. Thus, they emphasized their belief that mass, volume and surface were what constituted sculpture.

Op art

A rather odd relative of minimal was Op art, given this title as a result of the Museum of Modern Art's 1965 exhibition known as "The Responsive Eye." Op art was not so much a movement as a product of the studies of various artists in the science of vision. The Op artists were essentially minimalists or pure abstractionists, who found in their work with color and pattern that they could create images that seemed to move, or produce other deceptive effects. Some of the pictures created dizziness or afterimages. The Op show included Morris Louis, Ad Reinhardt, Kenneth Noland, Joseph Albers and others who had not thought of their work as being part of

Bridget Riley
Cataract V, 1967.
(Richard Feigen Gallery)

such a movement. However, the idea caught the public's fancy partly because, like Pop, it was "fun," and partly because it came at a time of interest in hallucinatory visual effects produced by "psychedelic" drugs. Op art fitted neatly into this scene and was almost instantly co-opted by the advertising and fashion business. Within weeks after the Museum of Modern Art show, young people were dancing in Op art shirts and dresses in the new "mixed-media" discotheques.

Art comes off its pedestal

The Sixties saw a revolutionary shift in the conception of what art should be, and a good deal of this change had to do with art objects in space rather than paint on canvas. Once upon a time sculpture had been identifiable as three-dimensional stationary objects of wood, stone, ceramic or metal, wrought by an artist's own hands and adhering to certain principles of balance and unity which usually gave them a look of stability and permanence.

Edward Kienholz
The Wait, 1965, mixed media construction.
(Dwan Gallery)

However, in 1913 (three years before the official birth of Dada), Marcel Duchamp introduced a bicycle wheel as an art object and upset all prevailing formulations. Here was a three-dimensional object, selected by an artist as sculpture, but not made by him. A later Dadaist, Kurt Schwitters, gathered the debris of contemporary society to make gigantic assemblages. And from that time on artists continued to experiment with "readymade" materials. The artists of the Fifties, in arranging their "junk" sculptures, including machine parts, bottles and household objects, began also to include mechanical and electronic devices—flashing lights and motorized parts. Sculpture, if it was still sculpture, seemed suddenly to become real, alive. It moved off its pedestal and became a form of theater or "environment."

One form of the new sculpture which came very close to theater was the carefully composed narrative tableau which evolved out of the assemblages of the Fifties. However, instead of creating an abstract composition out of coke bottles and machine parts, artists like Marisol, Ed Kienholz and George Segal combined real objects with modelled or painted forms into scenes which blended imaginative and documentary elements. Kienholz' "State Hospital," for example, presents two modelled figures of the same corpselike beaten man lying in duplicate actual cots of a reconstructed hospital room, complete with bare bedside table. Segal's "Gas Station" presented sterile emptiness, emphasized by a gas station attendant as anonymous as the tanks, a coke machine and three seated people, as unindividualized as the objects. Despite a lack of complexity or freshness of insights, these works had strong theatrical impact as social documentary. They were called mixed-media assemblages.

Light and movement

A very different kind of theater or environmental art was to grow out of the luminal and kinetic experiments beginning in the early Twenties with Thomas Wilfred's invention of a color organ for producing light patterns on a screen and Naum Gabo's motorized constructions. Over the years, experimenters using light, plexiglass discs and plastic screens explored the possibilities of luminal art. At the same time isolated artists were working with kinetic sculpture. Alexander Calder and Switzerland's Jean Tinguely were the only major artists to produce a substantial body of kinetic work, Calder creating mobiles which danced and turned by natural motion and Tinguely making complicated, motor-driven, fanciful machine sculptures. The Hungarian artist, Laszlo Moholy-Nagy, saw the affinity between light and motion and predicted in 1938 that kinetic sculpture projecting light patterns would eventually replace static art.

Whether this prediction will ever come to pass is still a question. But what was clear by the end of the Sixties was that luminal-kinetic art had a power to involve people on a sensory level that more static arts did not have. Artists such as Robert Rauschenberg, Robert Whitman, Allan Kaprow and Michael Kirby became fascinated not only by movement and light, but by films, TV, video tapes, electronically amplified sounds and the way people interact with these things. Such artists had no desire to create an object that people might simply look at. They wanted to create an environment that people entered and reacted to in some definite way. Some artists, such as Kaprow, became involved in "Happenings," events that gave participants the opportunity to interact with various materials like rubber tires (one might pile them in a heap) or burlap bags (why not put people in them and carry them to Grand Central Station?). But most became interested in such developments as the laser ray light, which could draw a pattern around a room, or fluorescent and neon lights, which might be used as sculptural and color elements, or electronic devices that converted sound into light patterns.

Günther Uecker
Zero Garden, 1966, nails on masonite.
(Howard Wise Gallery)

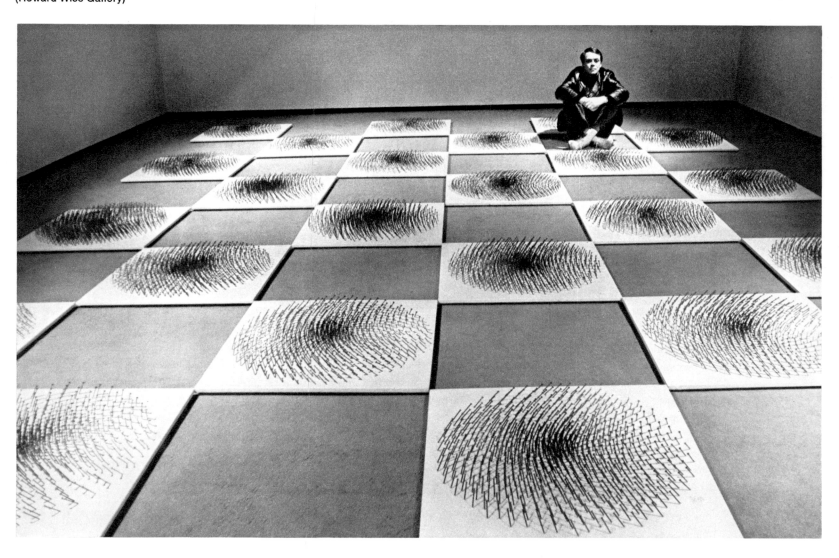

Steven Antonakos
Walk on Neon, 1968, neon light sculpture.
(Fischbach Gallery)

Enter technology

As the work of the artists with the new technology became more complex they began to seek help from scientists. Billy Klüver, a physicist connected with Bell Laboratory, who for years had aided Tinguely, helped to establish a rapport between artists and other scientists. The marriage of technology and art was celebrated in 1966 in an event, called "Nine Evenings of Art and Technology," that was one of the most successful failures of the decade: although the technology misbehaved and the art was never properly plugged in, it marked the founding of EAT —Experiments in Art and Technology— with Klüver and Rauschenberg as guiding spirits. The organization, designed to promote cooperation between artists and technologists, provided information and materials to artists and set up an exchange of ideas between artists and scientists.

A modish idea about art in the late Sixties was that it must relate in a new way to the techno-electronic era. A theory for what was already happening in the art world was provided by Marshall McLuhan's book, "Understanding Media." McLuhan's thesis was that the Gutenberg or print-oriented era had come to an end. For some four hundred years man's thinking had been shaped by the solitary, intellectual act of reading. In the new electronic age people, drawn together into a "global village" by TV and other electronic media, would become aurally rather than visually oriented. With aural orientation, according to McLuhan's philosophy, man becomes capable of taking in more than one thing at a time. It is not necessary to focus on a single thought and then move on to the next. In tribal society, art is not relegated to museums but is an aspect of religion and daily living, that is, members of the tribe dance, sing, paint themselves and their homes as part of ritual celebrations. In the new age, with all the world a part of one vast tribe, art will be restored to its ancient function. Avant-garde artists hailed McLuhan's ideas and found in the multimedia discotheque with its electronically amplified music, its flashing strobe lights, its barrage of films and light patterns screened on walls and patrons, and the dancing of the participants, something of a model for the contemporary art experience. Here was art becoming an aspect of life.

Whether or not the McLuhan formulation is sound remains to be seen. However, there was another aspect to the art scene of the Sixties. A tide of affluence had brought a new, educated managerial class to whom art was a status symbol. The dy-

namic curators of flourishing museums and the alert art dealers, faced with a hungry public and insatiable media, managed to discover new trends with each season. When Pop, Op and Minimal cooled off, light and light-and-sound switched on. Galleries promoted "air art," in which elasticized strings defined forms, and "earth art" featuring patterns created out of dirt. There were also "participation art" and "optional art" (shoots off the mixed-media tree), which required the viewer to push buttons and place materials in order to bring the work into being.

By the end of the Sixties New York had been the art capital of the world for twenty-five years and it was clear that the beat of the city of advertising, commerce and technology had, for better or worse, entered the blood stream of art.

Dan Flavin
Pink & Gold, 1968, neon light sculpture.
(Dwan Gallery)

Painting

Paul Jenkins. Phenomena
Devil's Footsteps, 1968.
Collection Frederick Weissman.
The delicate flow of paint
represents one of the differences between abstract
expressionism and the linear
sharpness of hard-edge
painting. (Martha Jackson Gallery)

Tom Wesselman (above). Gan No. 89, 1967.
Wesselman often turns to erotic subjects and uses a
photographer's cropping technique to focus attention.
(Sidney Janis Gallery)

James Brooks (right). Cullodon, 1967.
Revealing a debt to oriental calligraphy, Brooks
carries on in the abstract expressionist tradition.
(Martha Jackson Gallery)

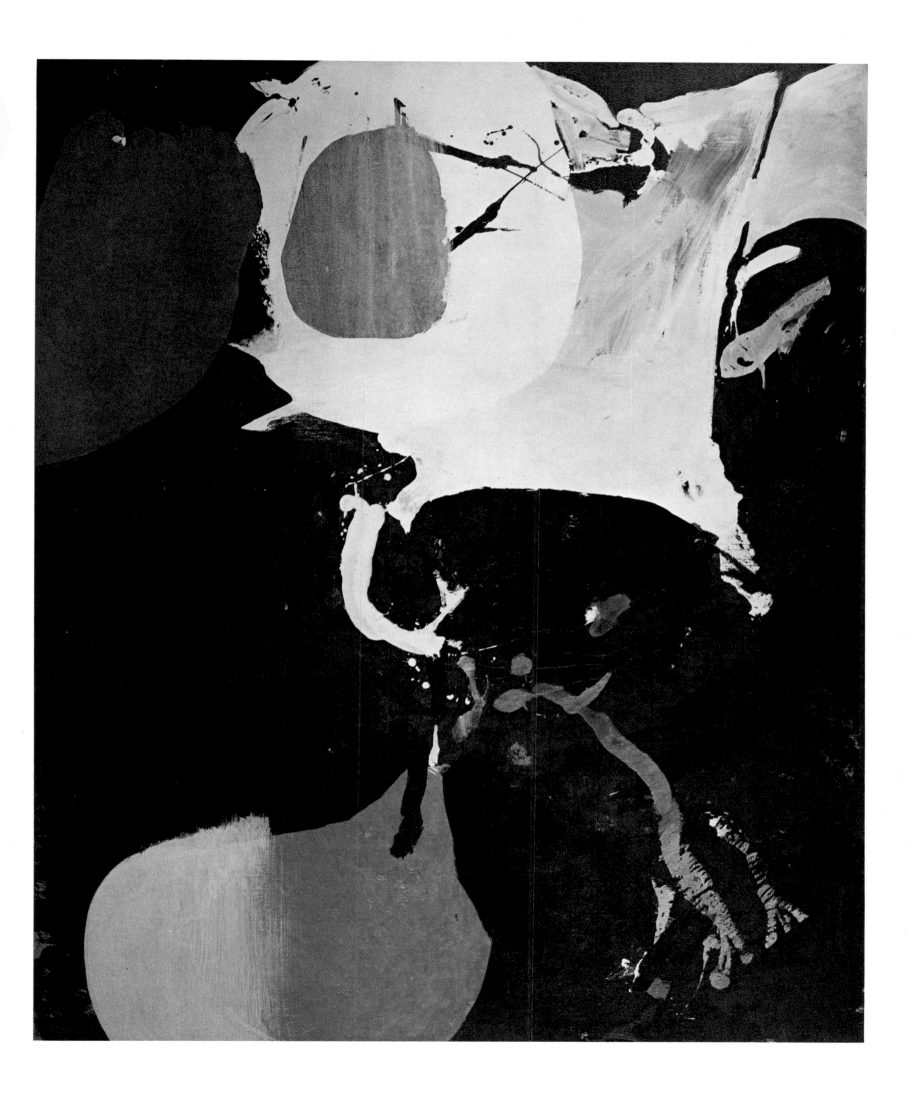

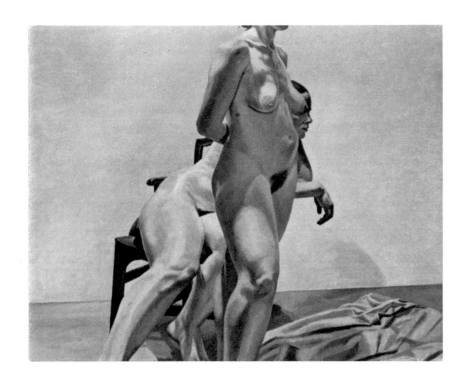

Philip Perlstein (left). Models in the Studio: One Standing, 1967.
With figures cropped as though they were part of an abstract design, this painting reveals a sculptor's concern with plane and volume. (Allan Frumkin Gallery)

Sidney Goodman (below). Self-Portrait in Studio, 1967.
The theme here, as in much of Goodman's work, is man's isolation and alienation. (Terry Dintenfass, Inc.)

Richard Lindner (right). Ice, 1966.
Holding up a mirror to our time, Lindner's paintings express brutality and repressed violence. (Whitney Museum of American Art, New York)

36

Willem de Kooning (left).The Visit, 1967.
Born in Holland, de Kooning has been a major
influence on painting since the Forties. He is the
only abstract expressionist who constantly uses
the human figure. (M. Knoedler & Co., Inc.)

Al Held (below). Mao, 1967.
In its simplification of elements, Held's recent work
parallels that of the minimal sculptors.
(André Emmerich Gallery)

Pierre Soulages. 21 September, 1967.
The broad, vigorous strokes used by
this leading French artist relate him to
the American Action painters.
(M. Knoedler & Co., Inc.)

Andrew Wyeth. The Country, 1965.
This portrait illustrates the qualities—
the lone figure in a familiar country
setting, the masterly draughtsmanship,
the sense of inner strength—that have
made Wyeth famous. (Virginia Museum
of Fine Arts)

Jack Youngerman (left above). Bahia, 1967.
The hard-edge treatment strongly identifies
Youngerman as a painter of the Sixties.
(Betty Parsons Gallery, New York)

Fritz Glarner (left below). Relational Painting:
Tondo 65, 1965.
Reminding us that ''shaped'' canvases are not
new, this Swiss painter uses the Renaissance
term ''tondo'' for a circular painting.
(Graham Gallery)

Helen Frankenthaler (right). The Human Edge, 1967.
This work exemplifies the bold contrasts this painter
achieves by means of strong color.
(André Emmerich Gallery)

Alex Katz (above). Ada Phoning, 1967.
Like that of many Pop artists, Katz's painting seems
to illustrate or tell a story.
(Fischbach Gallery)

Roy Lichtenstein. Drawing for Modern Painting of
New York State, 1968.
Experienced in outdoor advertising, Lichtenstein
delights in the exaggerated scale that surrounds us
in the form of billboards and marquee displays.
(Leo Castelli Gallery)

Oyvind Fahlstrom. Roulette, 1966.
Fahlstrom often attaches hinged or magnetized
movable parts to his canvas to create
"variable paintings." (Sidney Janis Gallery)

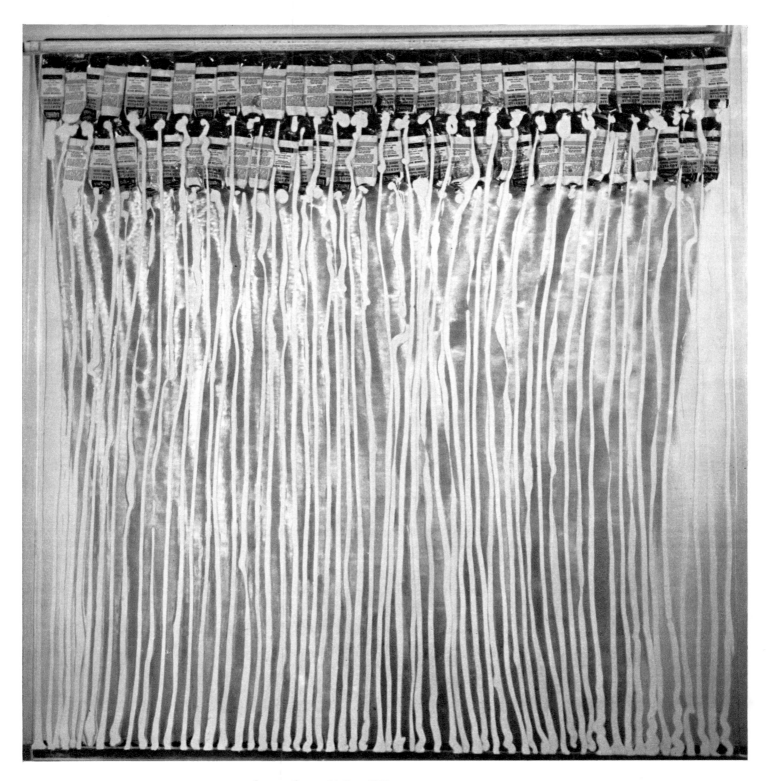

Arman. Squaw Valley, 1968.
A member of the European school of New
Realists, Arman builds his paintings out of a
collection of objects such as the paint tubes
used here. (Sidney Janis Gallery)

Richard Diebenkorn (left). Sleeping Woman, 1961. Diebenkorn continues to do paintings of figures and landscapes but has gradually abandoned the illusion of depth. (Poindexter Gallery)

Philip Guston (below). Untitled, 1967. An exceptional sensitivity to color marks Guston's highly lyrical work. (Marlborough-Gerson Gallery)

Francis Bacon (above). Portrait of George
Dyer and Lucien Freud, 1967.
Mutilated and macabre forms express this
English painter's view of man.
(Marlborough-Gerson Gallery)

Robert Motherwell (left). Spontaneity with
Blue Stripe, 1966.
A painting that seems, like so much of
Motherwell's work, to explore the symbolic
forms of the unconscious.
(Marlborough-Gerson Gallery)

Josef Albers (right below). Homage to the Square "Ascending." Once a member of the German Bauhaus movement devoted to functionalism in the arts, Albers is famous for the variations he has made of these squares within squares.
(Withney Museum of American Art, New York)

Mark Tobey. Incantation, 1966.
A member of the Pacific Coast group that includes Morris Graves, Tobey uses a calligraphic brushstroke that he calls "white writing."
(Willard Gallery)

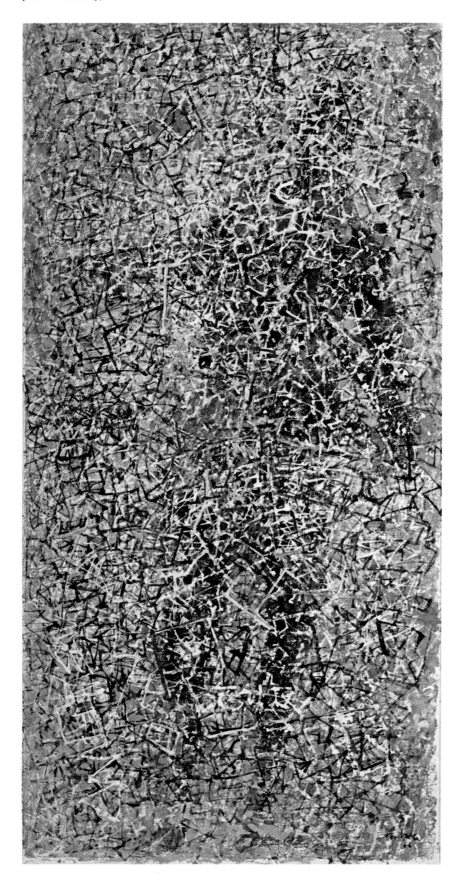

Grace Hartigan. Trick or Treat, 1965.
The heavy outlines of the shapes in this artist's
work are reminiscent of folk and children's
paintings as well as of stained glass.
(Martha Jackson Gallery)

Sculpture

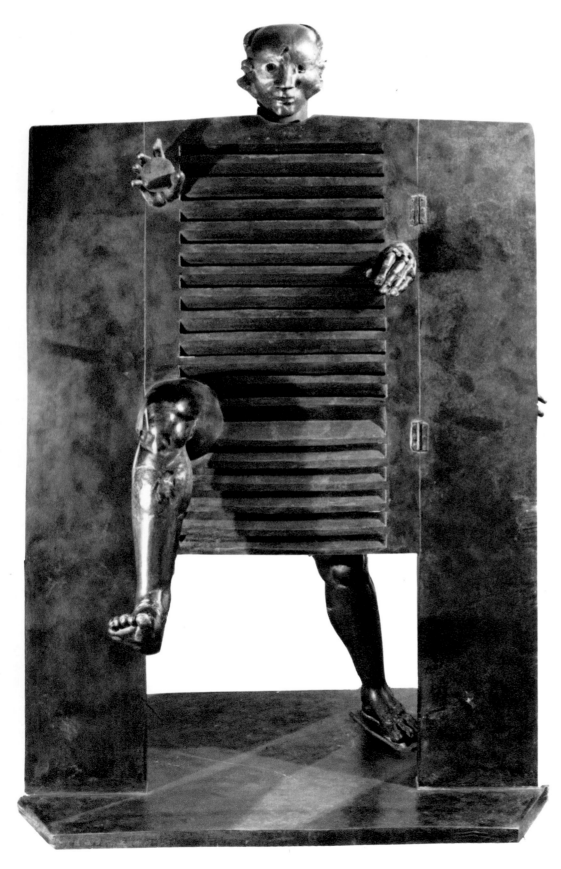

Jean-Robert Ipousteguy (left). Man Pushing a Door, 1966.
In his larger-than-life pieces, Ipousteguy dissects the human body and fuses it with objects in the environment. (Pierre Matisse Gallery)

Marisol (right). Dinner Date, 1962–1963.
Collection Mrs. Frederick Hilles. Once again this Venezuelan artist uses an almost exaggerated folk-like style to show average people in routine activities. (Stable Gallery)

Gio Pomodoro. III Guscio, 1966–1967.
Like much Italian sculpture since the Futurists, this
shows a concern with the fluidity and power of
machine forms. (Galleria dell'Ariete, Milan)

Forrest Myers (right). Ziggurat WWW, 1966.
Collection of Mr. and Mrs. Murchison, Dallas.
A minimal structure using aluminium with baked
epoxy and acrylic lacquer. (John Gibson Gallery)

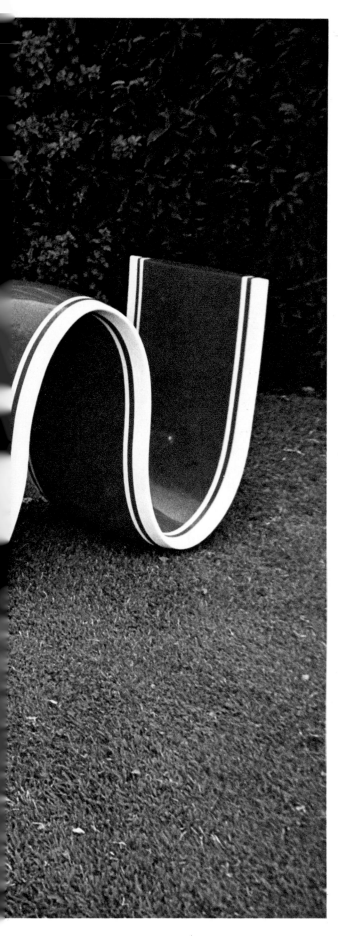

Mary Bauermeister. 308975 Times No, 1966.
A German-born sculptor here seals organic
bubbles in a frame within a frame.
(Galeria Bonino)

Richard Randell. Red & Orange Meander, 1967.
A typical example of Randell's playfulness on
a monumental scale. (Royal Marks Gallery)

George Segal. Segal Studio Shot, 1965.
In his tableaux, the artist "stops" everyday life with
anonymous figures in plaster of paris.
(Sidney Janis Gallery)

Jean Arp (left). Nid-Enchanteur, 1965.
One of the Old Masters of modern sculture,
Arp called his works "concretions," meaning
objects that have grown together as in nature.
(Sidney Janis Gallery)

Peter Agostini. Baby Doll and Big Daddy, 1967.
Inflated inner tubes, shaped and covered with
thick plaster, make up Agostini's "pneumatic
sculpture." (Stephen Radich Gallery)

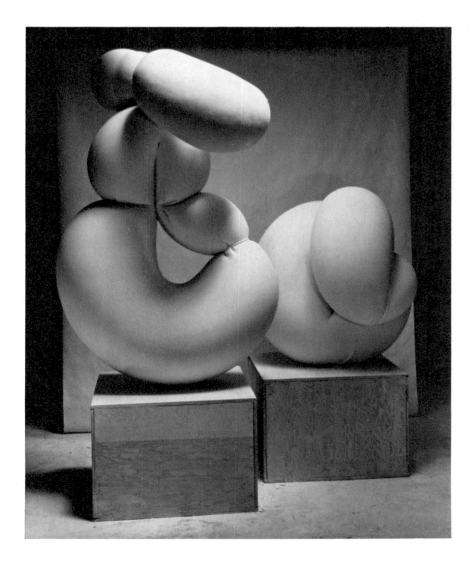

Kenneth Snelson. Audrey I, 1965.
Collection of John and Kimiko Powers.
Snelson employs engineering techniques learned as a student of architect-designer Buckminster Fuller.

José de Rivera. Construction No. 103, 1967. Collection Mr. Lionel Bauman. This piece, characteristic of de Rivera's work, exploits the tensile strength of metals. (Grace Borgenicht Gallery)

Mark de Suvero. Loveseat, 1965.
"Junk" objects carefully
selected and suspended in
space identify the work of this
young American sculptor.
(Dwan Gallery)

Henry Moore (left). Three Part Object. Collection Austin Briggs. This much-honored English sculptor maintains the tradition of direct carving and fidelity to materials that he admires in the work of the pre-Columbian, African and early Anglo-Saxon sculptors.

Alexander Calder. Seven-Footed Beastie. Collection Austin Briggs. Internationally recognized for his mobi es, Calder has long been an innovator in his handling of metal shapes.

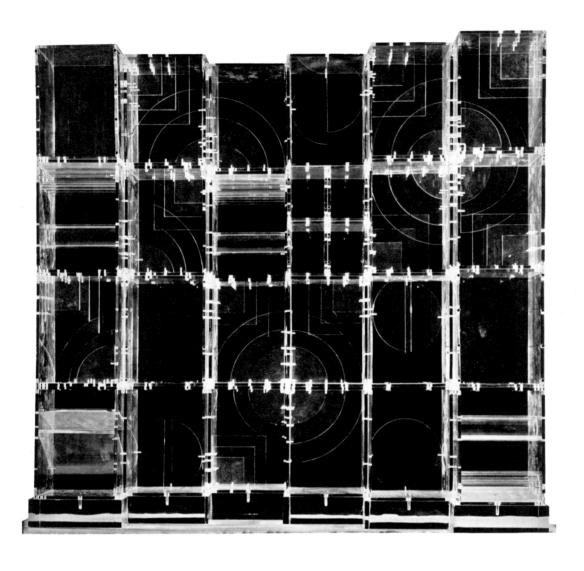

Louise Nevelson (left above). Model for Atmosphere and Environment, Ice Palace I, 1967. Another variation of the box shapes in wood, aluminum or plastic for which this artist has become known. (Pace Gallery)

Lee Bontecou (left). Untitled, 1966.
In spite of their enormous size, Miss Bontecou's stitched, shaped canvases retain something of the delicacy of a spider's web. (Leo Castelli Gallery)

Frank Gallo (right). Man at Desk, 1967. Collection Mr. and Mrs. Paul Hoffman, Illinois. A characteristic example of this artist's satiric view of the world of the "beautiful people."

Alicia Penalba (right). Triology, 1966.
Relying on traditional materials such as
bronze and stone, this Argentinian
artist creates jewel-like forms.
(Galeria Bonino)

Eduardo Chillida (below). Espace
Partagé, 1966–1967.
A complex interpenetration of planes
and squared-off volumes characterizes
the work of this Spanish artist.
(Galerie Maeght, Paris)

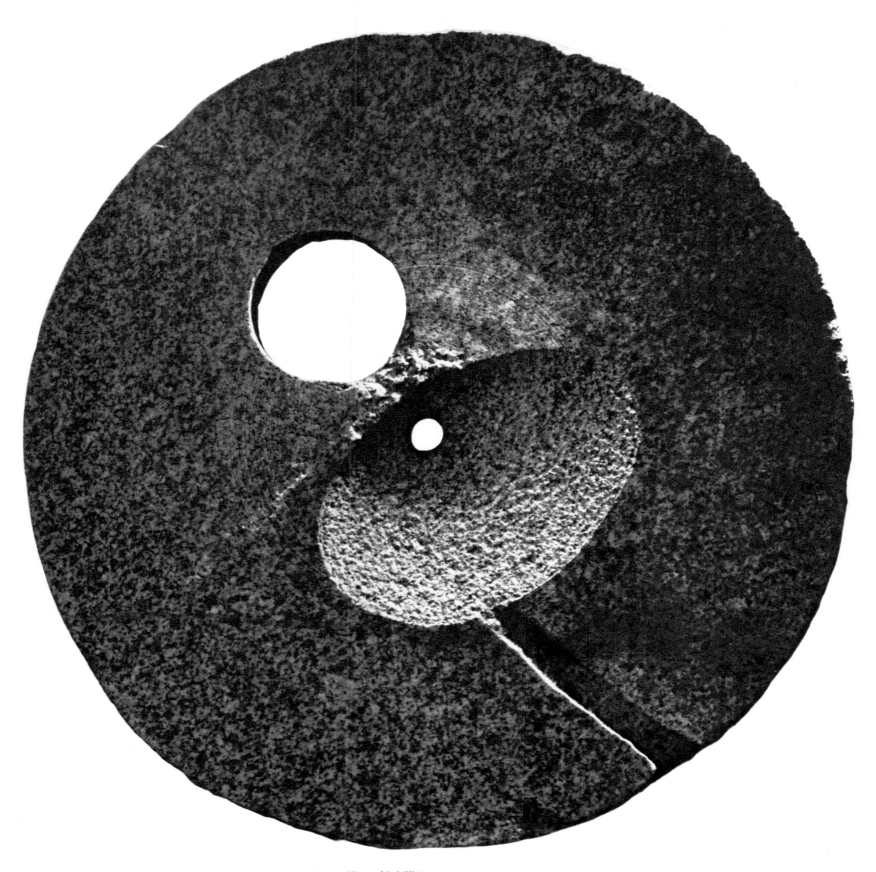

Isamu Noguchi. Millstone.
Collection Robert Benjamin. Noguchi
was one of the first sculptors to be
interested in natural materials and
minimal shapes.
(Cordier-Ekstrom Gallery)

Graphic Art

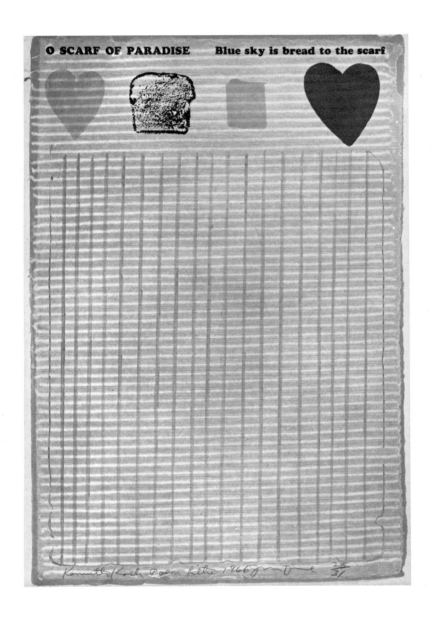

Jim Dine (left). Lithograph for a poem by Kenneth Koch.
Known for his "Happenings" and neo-Dada paintings, Dine here collaborates with a poet. (Universal Limited Art Editions)

Dennis Beall (above). The Big Eye. Typical of the Pop artist's detachment, this cyclopean eye draws the beholder as to a target. (Associated American Artists)

David Finkbeiner (left). Untitled landscape.
The use of embossed paper creates a sense
of thickness that causes the pictorial plane
simultaneously to advance and recede.
(Pratt Graphics Center)

Leonard Baskin (above). Young Mother.
An outstanding sculptor and graphic artist,
Baskin depicts tragedy with haunting depth of
expression. (Grace Borgenicht Gallery)

Lester Johnson (left above).
Bathers with Columns.
Johnson's lithographs
resemble his paintings in their
slashing configurations based on
the human form. (Martha Jackson
Gallery)

Albert Blaustein (left).
Kamatipura I.
Concentrating on somber subject
matter, this artist achieves a
Goya-like treatment of space and
chiaroscuro. (Associated
American Artists)

Antonio Frasconi (right).
The Hawks VII.
In this masterly, symbolic interpretation from his "Hawk" woodcut series, Frasconi dramatizes
contemporary man's plight.
(Brooklyn Museum)

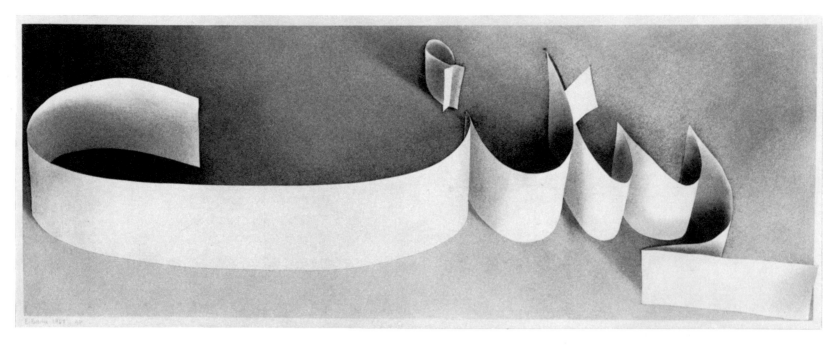

The Flood of Laymen

Kitaj

Edward Ruscha (far left above). Long City. This West Coast Pop artist constructs with icy precision his own version of the American industrial scene. (Alexander Iolas Gallery)

Ernest Trova (far left). Study: Falling Man. Well known for his "Falling Man" series, Trova continues to present man in robotized, featureless anonymity. (Brooklyn Museum)

R. B. Kitaj (left). The Flood of Laymen. Linked to Pop art, Kitaj depicts the everyday scene with a strong addition of the grotesque. (Marlborough-Gerson Gallery)

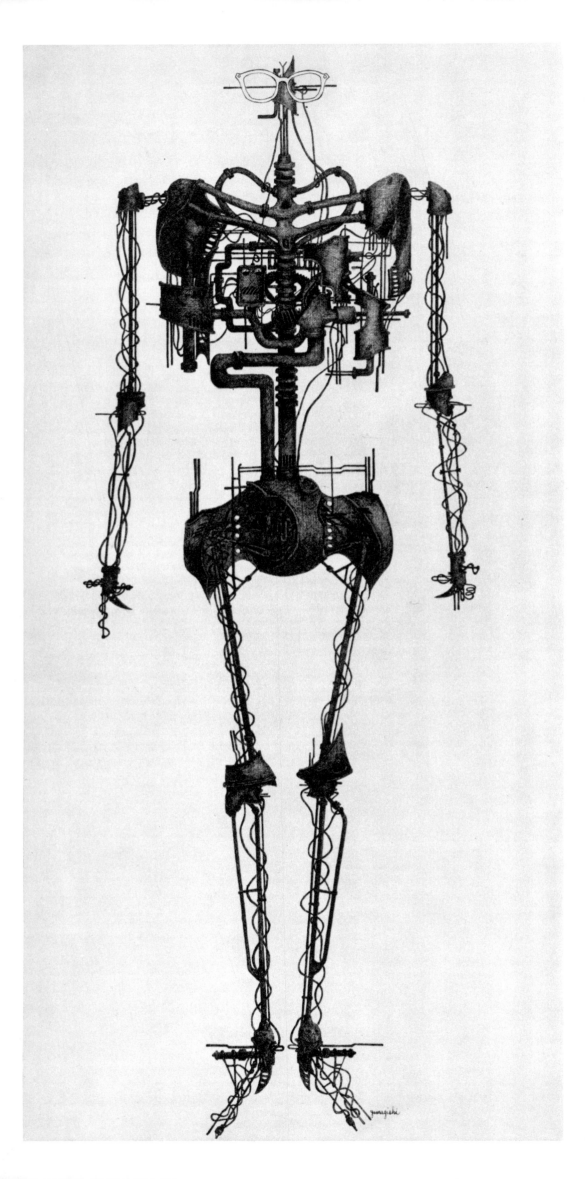

Yoshi Yamagishi (left). Silent World I.
A twenty-five-year-old Japanese artist represents the mechanized condition of man in
our time.

Marino Marini (right). Idea e Spazio.
A famous Italian sculptor, whose favorite
subject is the horse, here uses symbolism
with powerful linear directness.
(Martha Jackson Gallery)

Lee Bontecou (left). Etching One.
Characteristic of Miss Bontecou's bold
canvas-and-wire constructions, this etching
evokes the atmosphere of science fiction.
(Universal Limited Art Editions)

Will Barnet (above). Compression.
Primarily concerned with figurative painting,
Barnet here resumes his early exploration of
subtle balance in abstract design.
(Brooklyn Museum)

14/75

Robert Motherwell (left). Gauloises Bleues.
Leaving behind his audaciously experimental
"improvisations," this leading American
painter's aquatint suggests the witty, orderly
imagery of French collagists.
(Universal Limited Art Editions)

Higa. SIS-12.
Minimal, free-floating forms in spatial infinity
typify this Japanese artist's work.
(Pratt Graphics Center)

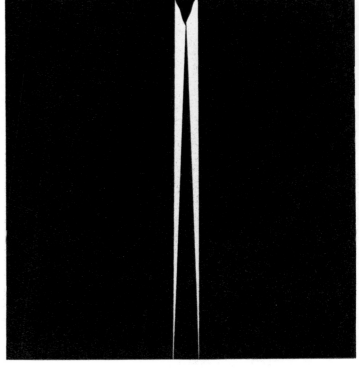

RAUSCHENBERG 6⁵/₄₀ 68

Robert Rauschenberg (left). Landmark.
A photomontage report of the fleeting moment
records this versatile innovator's view of a
changing world. (Universal Limited Art
Editions)

Esteban Vicente (right). Untitled.
Vicente's remarkable collages are adapted to
the lithograph stone, creating a dreamlike
suspension of abstract shapes. (Hallander
Workshop Gallery)

Carol Summers (below). Dark Rainbow.
Summers has devised an original approach,
unusual for the woodcut technique, to express
monumental visions in sumptuous colors.
(Associated American Artists)

3 The Uses of Art

The Art Director

by Allen F. Hurlburt

Last night, if you watched the close of a movie being rerun on television, and if you paused to look closely as the credits crawled up the screen, somewhere toward the end, between the titles of film editor and costume designer, you would have noticed the title of "Art Director." This is one of the rare times that an average person may encounter this title, but it represents only a fraction of the influence this group of professionals exerts.

Earlier the same evening you may have been persuaded to read an article because of the compelling graphic use of words and pictures engineered by the magazine art director. Or your wife may have altered a hemline based on the high-fashion photography and exciting visual presentation of a magazine page.

The car you drove home was probably purchased only after a decision influenced in many ways: by advertisements in magazines and newspapers, by commercials on television, or showroom catalogues. In all of these an art director played a role as designer and supervisor of the page, and often as creator or co-creator of the persuasive concept from which the advertising developed.

Some art director was directly or indirectly responsible for the design of the container of the toothpaste, and perhaps even the form and contour of the toothbrush itself, with which you ended the day. A day in which your were in some way impressed, pleased, soothed, bored or annoyed a hundred times by an art director's skill or his lack of it.

Together with artists, photographers, film-makers and typographers who work with him, the art director covers a broad range of modern communication materials and exerts a wide influence on the world we live in. When he is good, he can bring beauty, excitement and the quality we call "taste" into our lives. When he is not, he must share the responsibility for the irritation and imitation, the superficial and banal effects often evident in contemporary communication.

The art director is a catalyst in the communication process. Under his hand the printed page or film takes on its first resemblance to the finished form in which it will be viewed. His layout of the editorial or advertising space often closely approximates the final image and it provides the basis on which management decisions are made.

In the early days of art direction, when he assisted editors and advertising copy writers in the planning and processing of illustration, a sketchbook, a pencil and a certain skill at drawing were sufficient. Many of the early art directors were drawn from the ranks of frustrated painters and illustrators whose talents were not quite great enough to qualify them for the work they were trained for. Today, the art director is a trained specialist who often has studied in the graphic design departments of universities and art schools. He has frequently developed and refined his talent through graduate schools of design and professional extension courses. The art director learns very early in his career that for him the education process can never end.

To understand the comparatively new career of art directing we should examine some of the different kinds of art directors.

Impresario of the Ad

First there is the advertising art director. He will be found as often outside his office as in it. You may encounter him in the client meeting, the creative conference or the art gallery. You may see him on an early morning flight to Detroit sketching

Poster of Bob Dylan designed by Milton Glaser to be included in Columbia Records album. Art Director: John Berg

One of the earliest modes of advertising, posters were already an art form in Europe at the beginning of the century. In this country they were converted into billboards and car-cards without artistic value. Some years ago, college students began to collect European and offbeat American posters to hang on walls. Soon posters were being created not as advertising, but as pure wall decoration. The poster shown here retains a trace of its early use because it was designed for a Dylan record album, but its primary function is decoration.

layouts in the white space of someone else's ad in his copy of the morning paper, or on location with a photographer checking to be sure that the photographic approach and the camera view will mesh with his concept of the page design.

His office may be neat or cluttered, but it is always busy when he is there, and by the end of a day his oversize wastebasket is full of layouts and ideas discarded in the search for a newer and better approach. His telephone rings constantly, and in between there are countless artists' and photographers' portfolios to be studied in the hope of finding a fresh solution to recurring problems.

Where do the ideas come from? Most of them are hammered out in the frequent sessions between the art director and copy writer—the creative team. Some ideas stem from the collective creative conferences in a group encounter often referred to as "brain-storming." Sometimes they come out of thin air when least expected. Only on the rarest occasion are these ideas original. Usually they are a synthesis of past performance and existing appeals to which a twist has been added. Too often they are a mere paraphrase of someone else's idea.

The idea, once achieved, still has a rough road to travel before it reaches the printed page. After it is rendered into a rough or comprehensive layout (a reasonable facsimile of the final result), it must stand up to the account group, the plans board, and the client presentation. In the process it will be subject to the opinions of self-appointed experts and second-guessers ranging from the motivational research analysts to the client's Aunt Lucy. In the light of this ritual test of fire, it is surprising that advertising is as good as it is, and it is little wonder that the expression

"back to the old drawing board" is so familiar in the art departments of advertising agencies.

Television's Time Manipulator

With increasing frequency the agency art director who designs for the printed page is also responsible for television commercials. In a few agencies he is a separate specialist trained in film-making and theatrical production. Where the layout serves as a plan for the printed page, the story-board is the guide for the commercial. A story-board is a series of sketches laid out in a comic strip form that describes in still images the progression that will make up the final film continuity.

Each year advertisers spend more than three billion dollars on television commercials. These compressed-time capsules crowd an impressive quantity of salesmanship into anywhere from ten seconds to one minute of expensive running time. They cost an average of $22,000 per minute to produce, and their quality ranges from exciting entertainment to ultimate boredom.

In a review of TV commercials Time magazine remarked: "Commercials are infuriating. They are also irresistable. Commercials are an outrageous nuisance. They are also apt to be better than the programs they interrupt. Commercials are the heavy tribute that the viewer must pay to the sponsor in exchange for often dubious pleasure. They are also an American art form. A minor art form, but the ultimate in mixed media: sight, sound and sell."

The story-board is only a first step in this vast creative effort. The art director is also involved in the selection and supervision of the film producers, acting talent,

Clairol fashion advertising, with photography by Richard Avedon. Art Director Chuck Bua for the Douglas D. Simon agency.

It is increasingly difficult to make an advertisement stand out in the competition of the so-called high style magazines. This layout does so by incorporating seven different photographs and by careful cropping, variation in scale, and an unusual overall concept.

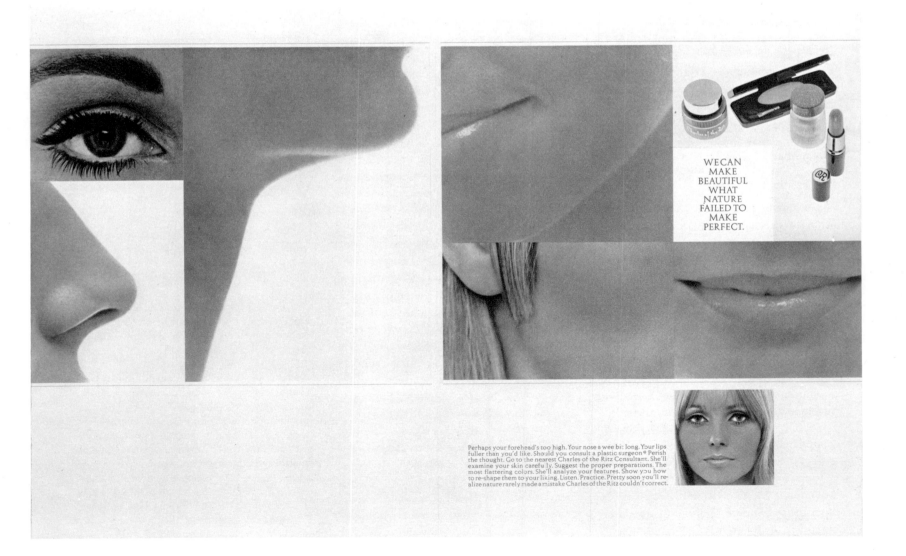

WE CAN MAKE BEAUTIFUL WHAT NATURE FAILED TO MAKE PERFECT.

Perhaps your forehead's too high. Your nose a wee bit long. Your lips fuller than you'd like. Should you consult a plastic surgeon? Perish the thought. Go to the nearest Charles of the Ritz Consultant. She'll examine your skin carefully. Suggest the proper preparations. The most flattering colors. She'll analyze your features. Show you how to re-shape them to your liking. Listen. Practice. Pretty soon you'll realize nature rarely made a mistake Charles of the Ritz couldn't correct.

composers, sound engineers, animators, and special effects men who will turn out his miniature epic. The art director brought up on simple layout sheets and a 4-B pencil would be puzzled to discover his modern-day counterpart at the controls of a movieola. This elaborate projection machine that permits the operator to intermix sound and images against stopwatch timing is only one of the new creative tools many art directors are learning to cope with.

One needs only to look at contemporary movies to realize how many cinematic ideas have been borrowed from the time-compressing techniques developed for television with its quick cuts, stop-motion and subliminal effects. The peculiar quality that director Richard Lester brought to his movie "A Hard Day's Night" was directly traceable to his experience in producing more than three hundred TV commercials.

Publication Art Director

The magazine art director came into being when the revolution in the printing art brought sophisticated pictorial reproduction to the printed page. Editors who first tried to cope with the growing demand for visual images soon realized that they needed help in this area. This new editorial assistant was originally called an art editor, and his main function was to aid the editor in commissioning illustrations and arranging and cropping occasional photographs. As pictorial opportunities developed and increasing amounts of visual material were used, the art editor's role became more important and his title changed to art director.

Today's magazine art director is often the number-two man on the staff. As in other areas of contemporary design, his responsibility extends well beyond the arranging of elements on the printed page and he is frequently involved in editorial decisions far beyond the limits of the drawing board.

The first thing most magazines do when they are in trouble is replace the art director in the hope that the magic or the pyrotechnics of a new format will somehow solve all their problems. This dubious tribute to the importance of the magazine art director rarely works. In most cases it succeeds only in confusing the reader and focusing attention on the weakness of the editorial approach. Good design can make a significant contribution to a magazine's success but it cannot serve as a substitute for content and ideas, nor can it camouflage a mediocre product.

The measure of a magazine art director's success is often his ability to work with other people. Most well-designed magazines are the result of a close collaboration of the editor and the art director, and most of the truly effective pages result from an equally close collaboration between the art director and the illustrator or photographer.

The magazine world resembles an iceberg. The colorful consumer magazines that decorate the newsstands are the upper visual portion, but beneath these hundred or so publications are another thirty thousand business and professional publications. Many of these exist without art direction except on an occasional consulting basis, but there are an impressive number that are well designed and handsomely illustrated publications.

If the magazine field resembles an iceberg, so then does the entire area of art direction. Wherever goods and services are being promoted and sold, design has become a major factor. Throughout the communication and information industry, you will find art directors working on

Three ads from a Volkswagen campaign. Original Art Directors: Helmut Krone for Volkswagen, and George Gomes and Roy Grace for the Doyle Dane Bernbach agency.

These advertisements demonstrate the effectiveness of an interesting concept presented in a simple and direct form. In one ad the car was dropped gently on the surface of an especially constructed pool and photographed with an underwater camera to demonstrate a unique protective feature. Another ad stresses dependability by showing a defective Volkswagen dramatically destroyed before it leaves the assembly line. The third ad uses humorous art work and a stuttering headline to promote air conditioning as a new option.

Volkswagen's unique construction keeps dampness out.

For years there have been rumors about floating Volkswagens. (The photographer claims this one stayed up for about 42 minutes.)

Why not?

The bottom of the VW isn't like ordinary car bottoms. A sheet of flat steel runs under the car, sealing the bottom fore and aft.

That's not done to make a bad boat out of it, just a better car. The sealed bottom protects a VW from water, dirt and salt. All the nasty things on the road that eventually eat up a car.

The top part of a Volkswagen is also very seaworthy. It's practically airtight. So airtight that it's hard to close the door without rolling down the window just a little bit.

But there's still one thing to keep in mind if you own a Volkswagen. Even if it could definitely float, it couldn't float indefinitely.

So drive around the big puddles. Especially if they're big enough to have a name.

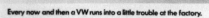

Every now and then a VW runs into a little trouble at the factory.

That hunk of junk was well on its way to being a Volkswagen, when it ran into a stone wall; a bunch of hard-nosed inspectors who pull enough parts off the line every day to make the equivalent of 30 cars. Or 2 freight cars full of scrap.

There are thousands of inspectors who literally pick every Volkswagen to pieces, every step of the way.

If there's a little scratch in a fender, it gets scratched. If there's a little nick in a bumper, it gets bumped.

Wherever ten people are doing something, there's an inspector to undo it. For the paint job alone, no less than 8 inspectors check every VW.

All that inspection doesn't mean the work isn't done carefully. The men who make the VW make it very well. The inspectors just make it perfect.

V-V-Volkswagen announces air conditioning.

Along with every air-cooled VW engine you can now get an air-cooled VW 100-HP, of course, is not exactly the kind of news that's going to stun the automotive industry.

But what is nice to know is that a 4-speed VW with a 3-speed air conditioner will only cost you a little over $2,000.

(The average car sold today with just a heater goes for $3,000.)

Air conditioning is one of approximately 50 optional accessories made especially for our cars.

For all bugs we have ski racks.

For music bugs, the luxury of an FM-AM radio.

For travel bugs, clothes hangers and mud flaps.

And where, you may ask, may all these princely pleasures be found?

At any Volkswagen dealer's.

Where else could you step into a $2,000 automobile and get a breath of fresh air?

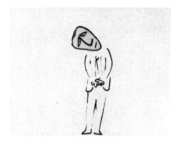

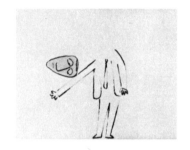

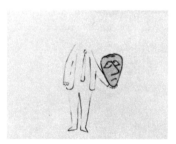

Alka-Seltzer

record albums, displays, packages and sales promotion campaigns. Whenever you pick up a book, whether it's a paperback book, an encyclopedia, or a limited edition, you will sense the influence of the graphic designer and art director. In the exploding educational field, design plays a part in everything from textbooks to programmed teaching materials and films.

The Corporate Designer

For many years, corporations looked at design as something expensive and perhaps wasteful, or as a necessary evil that the advertising agency insisted would aid the corporation's sales effort. The only place it encountered an art director was in the client meeting, and whatever design service it required was supplied by the agency. Gradually, under the leadership of enlightened corporations like Container, CBS and IBM, companies became aware of the need for an arbiter of taste within their own structures. To meet this need, they first turned to independent design organizations and finally set up their own design departments under a corporate art director.

The corporate art director has a broad range of responsibility. He is not only the guardian of the trademark and the tender of the corporate image, but he must concern himself with everything from the saleability of the product to letterheads, architecture, displays and office interiors. He is most successful when he bases his approach on a projection of the existing personality of his corporation, and least successful when he imposes his own design viewpoint without regard for the inherent nature of the company he serves.

TV Commercials for Alka-Seltzer. The strip at the left is an animated cartoon by William Steig; the other a movie short. Both prepared by Jack Tinker & Partners Inc., with George D'Amato and John Danza as art directors.

The strip at the left, visually simple, is animated with a detached and wobbling head. The voice explains that Alka-Seltzer has invented a new ailment called the "Blahs . . . kinda like the blues . . . only physical." The other commercial is like a feature film that must be completed in less than a minute. The action is built around a farcical pie-eating contest produced by Howard Zieff and it advises the viewer "to take what the guys who overeat for a living take next time you overeat."

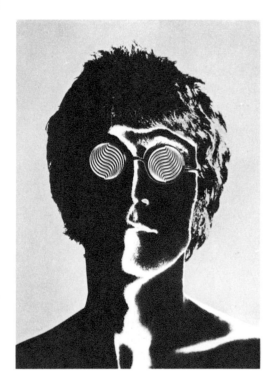

Photographs of the Beatles made by Richard
Avedon for Look Magazine.
Art Director: Allen F. Hurlburt

In a time of multimedia art, even the photographic still is molded to reflect the times. The
assignment began with discussions between
the photographer, art director and writer. This
was followed by nearly four months of experi-
mentation with the black and white negatives
using reversals, conversions and solarization,
and finally conversion to color through the
dye transfer process. The result was thus a
product of a collaboration between photographer, art director, and photographic
technicians.

Illustration entitled "The Maze" by Robert Vickery, an artist as well-known to the galleries as to magazine pages, for Redbook Magazine. Art Director: William Cadge

Image-Maker for Films

The film art director is something else again. His profession grew out of theatrical stage design and his background is more scenic than graphic. The need for him became evident when early film-makers conceived "epic" productions where a sense of history had to blend into set design on a heroic scale unimagined on the stage.

His talents are varied. He must be aware of the potentials and limitations of the camera and the magic that can be created by the special effects department. He must be part engineer, part architect, part interior decorator, part art historian and part costume designer. With all this, he has to be able to express himself with drawings and sketches that his director and producer can comprehend.

You may find the film art director in his Beverly Hills studio sketching an elabo-

rate scene for a first century triumphal entry into Rome, or touring the Cornish coast in a helicopter to find a setting sufficiently free of power wires and TV antennas to serve as a background for the filming of a nineteenth century novel. You may find him exploring the scientific accuracy of a giant centrifuge in outer space or supervising a reconstruction of Stonehenge. To cope with such a diversity of problems he usually needs a large staff of technicians, and he must often face a harrowing budget headache.

Although the title of art director has been in use since the 1920's, some critics believe that in the light of his assignments and his performance, both halves of the title are presumptuous. The title most generally suggested in its stead is designer: advertising designer, graphic designer, publication designer, film designer, etc. But these titles are also confusing

90

the Outrageous

"There's only one thing that really means anything to me and that's the Hell's Angels patch I wear. I can get me anything else—a new bike, a new old lady or money—but I can't get me another patch." "We've had a few deaths this year, but otherwise, it's been a good year. By that I mean we haven't had much police harassment." "It's like being brothers. Like, every man in the club's your brother." "Power. That's what it feels like when we ride in. On a three-day weekend, we might have one-fifty, two-hundred bikes out on a run. People all get excited when they see us coming, and—I don't know—it's beautiful." "You know what it is: it's a mind-blower. They come around with movie cameras. It's really beautiful." "If somebody messed up one of our brothers, it would be complete retaliation. An eye for an eye." "My brothers, that's my whole life. My brothers. It's all I've got." continued

and it is likely that the title of art director will be around for quite a while.

If the art director has failed to close the gap between life and art, if he has been quicker to imitate than originate, if he has been more of a huckster than a communicator, he has at least on occasion brought a glimpse of art, understanding and taste to our fast-changing environment. To meet the future, he will have to be better educated in the humanities and social sciences and better trained in his art. If, as Marshall McLuhan suggests, advertising will supply future historians with "the richest and most faithful daily reflections that any society has ever made of its entire range of activities," this revelation will probably first be felt in the influence of advertising on the more permanent art forms that surround it. Not only has film already embraced many of the techniques and much of the content of TV commercials, but through the medium of Pop art both painting and sculpture have exploited some of its more colorful and vulgar manifestations, as in AndyWarhol's Brillo boxes and Campbell soup cans, Roy Lichtenstein's enlarged halftone dots, and Claes Oldenburg's giant, sprawling imitations of objects and products.

Perhaps a more meaningful measure of the art director's contribution will be found in the social values of his work. It is increasingly evident that the communicator can no longer be content with his art and the simple accomplishment of his craft. His horizons must extend to a better understanding of his environment and the human relationships that form the background of all communication. He has an obligation, if he will only recognize it, to avoid the shoddy and the vulgar and to use all the powers and gifts of the talented men he works with.

Photograph by Irving Penn of "Hell's Angels" for a picture portfolio, "The Incredibles," in Look Magazine. Art Director: Allen F. Hurlburt.

This photograph is one of a portfolio by Irving Penn showing the revolutionary life styles developing in the San Francisco area: hippies, various singing groups, and the violent "Hell's Angels." The technique of direct confrontation between subject and camera was originally developed by Penn in photographing primitive people. The photograph looks disarmingly simple, but it was an incredibly difficult assignment to get these activists into such a studied pose.

Design elements for the Columbia
Broadcasting Company office building.
Director of Design: Lou Dorfsman

The director of design for a large corporation often has an astonishing variety
of functions. The illustrations on these
pages show a few of the problems faced
by the Director of Design of Columbia
Broadcasting when his firm moved into
its new Saarinen-designed Manhattan
office building (left). They represent,
first, the graphic identification of the
building, second, a three-dimensional
mural for the employee cafeteria that
makes playful use of graphic ideas, and
third, a clock designed to blend with
the other design elements.

Sketch for a scene in the MGM production of
"The Shoes of the Fisherman." Art Directors:
Eduard Carfagno and George Davis

This scene, one of dozens of sketches made
to guide the production, is the Sistine Chapel
of the Vatican, which had to be recreated on
a sound stage in Rome. Although the use of
clever photographic angles spared the need
to copy Michelangelo's ceiling, the reconstruction did involve a large portion of the monumental "Last Judgment" and several of the
huge frescoes painted by other sixteenth century masters for the walls of the chapel below
the ceiling. On the right two stills from the
film show how the production followed the
sketches.

Magazine Illustration

Magazine illustration mirrors our time and its arts. An illustrator must not only understand the temper of the age but have a grasp of all the techniques and styles—abstractions, collages, dayglo color, photomontage, Op Art and so forth—that are popular today. Where once an art director told the artist—sometimes in minute detail—how to illustrate a scene or article, today he may well leave it to the artist to enrich the text through his own vision or interpretation. The result is a less stilted and conventional kind of illustration and more individualized and sometimes strikingly fanciful work. In the best examples the illustrator adds a new dimension to the text. This tendency also brings illustration and freely creative painting closer together and in some instances fuses them.

Artist. Paul Hogarth (left)
Art Director. H. O. Diamond
Publication. The Lamp

Artist. Norman Rockwell (right)
Art Director. Allen F. Hurlburt
Publication. Look Magazine

norman rockwell

Artist. James Barkley (left)
"Mother of Loneliness"
Experiment in illustration

Artist. Paul Jasmin (left below)
Art Director. Samuel N. Antupit
Publication. Esquire Magazine

Artist. Simms Taback (below)
Art Director. Herb Lubalin
Publication. Avant Garde

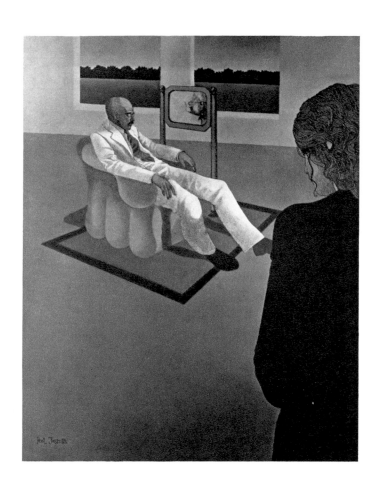

98

It would be of great service to all of us if you were to present the problem of world peace in the light of your most recent psychological discoveries, for such a presentation might well blaze the trail for new and fruitful modes of action. The ill succeed despite their obvious sincerity if all the efforts made during the last decade to reach this goal leaves us no room to doubt that strong psychological factors are at work.

Artist. Kinuko Craft (left)
Art Director. Don Zolweg
Book Title. The Big Abzul-Raider Game
Publisher. Science Research Associates, Inc.

Artist. Mark English (right above)
Art Director. Herbert Bleiweiss
Publication. Ladies Home Journal

Artist. Daniel Schwartz (right below)
Art Director. Samuel N. Antupit
Publication. Esquire Magazine

Artist. Bill Charmatz (far left)
Art Director. H. O. Diamond
Publication. The Lamp

Artist. Isadore Seltzer (left)
Art Director. Alvin Grossman
Publication. Venture Magazine

Artist. Charles Saxon (right)
Art Director. Otto Storch
Publication. McCall's Magazine

Artist. James McMullan (left)
Art Director. Walter H. Allner
Publication. Fortune Magazine

Artist. Fred Otnes (below)
Art Director. Asger Jerrild
Publication. Saturday Evening Post

Artist. Austin Briggs (right)
Art Director. Allen F. Hurlburt
Publication. Look Magazine

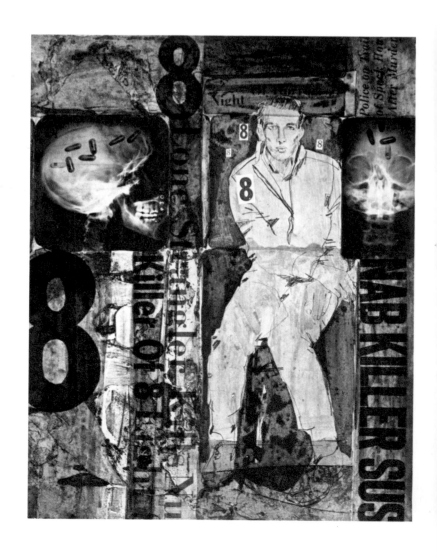

Artist. André François (right)
Art Director. H. O. Diamond
Publication. The Lamp

Artist. Robert Peak (below)
Art Director. Alvin Grossman
Publication. Venture Magazine

106

Artist. Lemuel Line (left)
Art Director. Samuel Antupit
Publication. Esquire Magazine

Artist. Austin Briggs (above)
Art Director. Robert Hallock
Publication. Lithopinion

Artist. Robert Weaver (right)
Art Director. Arthur Paul
Publication. Playboy Magazine

Artist. Jean-Paul Goude (left)
Art Director. Samuel Antupit
Publication. Esquire Magazine

Artist. Robert A. Heindel (above)
Art Director. Gery Colby
Client. Detroit Red Wings

Artist. Gilbert Stone (right)
Art Director. Richard Gangel
Publication. Sports Illustrated © Time Inc.

TOP
HUNT IN
THE
TOP END

BY VIRGINIA KRAFT

Civilization abruptly stops at Darwin in Australia's Northern Territory. There the bush takes over, and dirt tracks wander through a rough land abounding in beauty for the explorer and game for the hunter and fisherman

CONTINUED

93

Advertising Illustration

The art work in printed advertising grows more varied with each passing season. The aim is, as always, to attract attention and then make the advertised object seem as appealing and desirable as possible. Whatever special qualities the art itself has—elegance, humor, novelty, charm—will not only hold attention but be associated with the product. The best artists have a quality of their own but, as is evident in the following pages, they also draw inspiration and effects from all the studio arts of our time.

There are many rules for making good advertising art but some of the best pieces break the rules in order to achieve freshness and surprise. Sometimes there are so many factors to be considered that it takes a team, including an art director and a product expert, to achieve the right balance, but often it is still the artist who gives an outstanding piece of advertising art its special distinction.

Between Ellen and Jill came Paul.

SANDY DENNIS

KEIR DULLEA

ANNE HEYWOOD AS ELLEN MARCH

IN D. H. LAWRENCE'S

THE FOX

Artists. Leo and Diane Dillon (far left)
Art Directors. Tal Stiebis and John Wanek
Agency. Bill Gold Advertising, Inc.
Client. Warner Bros.—Seven Arts, Inc.

Artist. Ken Dallison (left)
Agency. Stewart and Caprarus Associates
Client. Honda

Artist. Robert Peak
Art Director. Robert Forgione
Agency. William Esty Co.
Client. Winston Cigarettes

The Antkeeper

WRITTEN AND DIRECTED BY
ROLF FORSBERG
AUTHOR OF "PARABLE"

PRODUCED BY THE LUTHERAN CHURCH IN AMERICA

WNDU-TV, CHANNEL 16
12 NOON (CST) FRIDAY, APRIL 12
COUNCIL OF CHURCHES OF ST. JOSEPH COUNTY

Artist. Reynold Ruffins
Art Director. Stanley White
Agency. Stanley White Studios
Client. The Lutheran Church in America

Plump

The ugly, five-letter word.

If you or someone in your family is a little plump, do something about it with Pine State's low calorie foods. Trim milk: tastes just like other milk, except we take the calories out and put more vitamins in. Trim Cottage Cheese: best thing going for a quick, light lunch. Tropi-Cal-Lo fruit drink: in fresh fruit flavors of orange and grape. Chocolate-flavored Instant Breakfast: only 168 calories when mixed with a glass of Trim milk. So if someone in your family needs to slim down, just flip the page, fill out the order form for your milkman, and we'll deliver.

Artist. John Alcorn (left)
Art Director. Charles McKinney
Agency. J. T. Howard Advertising
Client. Pine State's Low Calorie Foods

Artist. Charles Santore (right)
Art Director. Richard Herdegen
Agency. Ross Roy of New York, Inc.
Client. ITT Rayonier Inc.

AVRIL

THE ELECTRIC CIRCUS

THE ULTIMATE LEGAL ENTERTAINMENT EXPERIENCE

SAINT MARKS PLACE, BETWEEN 2ND & 3RD, EAST VILLAGE, N.Y.C.

Artist/Art Director. Jacqui Morgan (left)
Agency. Brownstone Associates
Client. Electric Circus

Artist/Art Director. Grace McQueen (right)
Agency. Warwick & Legler, Inc.
Client. Motown Productions, Inc.

Artist. Robert Blechman (above)
Art Director. Lou Portuesi
Client. Reader's Digest

Artist. Dorothy Michaelson (left)
Art Director. Dorothy Melze
Client. Neiman-Marcus

Stills from the film
The Yellow Submarine.
From Look Magazine © 1968,
Cowles Communications, Inc.

Artist. John Janus
Art Director. Tom Clemente
Client. Bureau of Advertising of the ANPA

Artist. Dorothy Renning
Art Director. Ron Firebough
Client. Neiman-Marcus

If you were
Loretta Young
Truman Capote
Buffy
Maria Von Trapp
Rex Reed
Astronaut James Lovell
Bill Blass
Gloria Vanderbilt
Senator Everett Dirksen
The Smothers Brothers
Danny Kaye
Tom Wolfe . . .

How would you decorate a Christmas tree for N-M?

Come see tomorrow, as we greet the holiday season decorated in typical N-M style! It wouldn't be nearly as merry if we didn't share it with friends . . . so we invited some marvelously talented people to decorate twelve Christmas trees for us. (Can you match celebrity to motif here? Clip the ad and see how well you do.) Discover the trees throughout the downtown store soaring with imagination – unlike any you've ever seen before. The unexpected. The enchanting. The clever. The beautiful. Christmas 1968 will never happen again – enjoy it to the fullest at N-M!

Neiman-Marcus

LUNE

Posters

Posters first attracted attention when famous Paris cafes and dance halls like the Moulin Rouge began to have outstanding artists such as Henri Toulouse-Lautrec make lithographs for them. The best of these early posters are today considered as much works of art as are paintings. In time, posters became another form of commercial advertising throughout Europe and America. But the appeal of travel and art exhibition posters also made them increasingly popular as wall decoration. Then about ten years ago artists began to make posters especially for wall decoration and soon established these lithographs as an independent art form, selling directly to the public. Free to be as colorful, arresting or even as shocking as it may, the poster has become an exciting new medium for the artist.

Big Nudes

Visual Arts Gallery
209 East 23rd Street
New York City

>{American Paintings from The Metropolitan Museum of Art}«

Los Angeles County Museum of Art   Lytton Gallery   June 3 - July 31, 1966

is the first letter of the alphabet
there are twenty-five more
the chicago public library has all of them
in some very interesting combinations

Artist. Milton Glaser (far left)
Art Director. Silas Rhodes
School of Visual Arts

Artist/Art Director. Louis Danziger (left)
Los Angeles Museum of Art

Artist. John Rieben (above)
Art Director. John Massey
City of Chicago

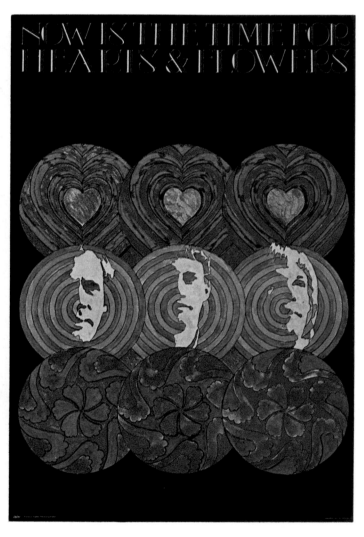

Artist/Art Director. James Gilbert (below left)
The Art Staff

Artist. John Van Hammersveld (below)
Art Director. George Osaki
Capitol Records, Inc.

Artist/Art Director. Peter Max (right)
Peter Max Poster Corp.

Overleaf:
Artist/Art Director. Herbert Leupin (left)
The Coca Cola Co.

Artist/Art Director. Lionel Kalish (right)
Cullen Rapp, Inc.

Pages 132–133:
Artist. Robert Cunningham
Art Director. Robert Brandwein
New York Racing Association

Pages 134–135:
Artist/Art Director. Tomi Ungerer (left)
Bookmasters

Artist. Al Parker (right)
Art Director. Robert Hallock
Lithopinion

128

Big, Bold, Be

autiful-Big A

EXHIBITION COVERS A.PARKER GRAPHIC EXPLORATIONS SOCIETY OF ILLUSTRATORS

FEB. 21 THROUGH MAR. 15

From LITHOPINION...also: Austin Briggs, Betty Fraser, Homer Hill, Joseph Low, Fred Otnes, Savignac, Noel Sickles, Bud Simpson and Tomi Ungerer

Children's Books

Children's books have offered a rich field for artists ever since the publication of Tenniel's illustrations for "Alice's Adventures in Wonderland" and the popular boys'-book drawings by Arthur Rackham and Howard Pyle. Books give an artist the unusual opportunity to carry through a whole series of illustrations or to do both the text and the illustrations himself.

With the explosion that has taken place in education, children's-book publishers have expanded spectacularly. The more enterprising publishers are allowing far greater latitude to artists than ever before, encouraging highly personal and even fanciful styles. Out of this has come some of the most charming, original and imaginative illustration work being done today.

Artist. Brian Wildsmith (below)
Book. Birds
Franklin Watts, Inc.

Artist. Tomi Ungerer (right)
Book. Moon Man
Harper & Row

Artist. Ellen Raskin (above)
Book. Spectacles
Atheneum Publishers

Artist. Leo Leonni
Book. Frederick
Pantheon Books

Artist. Ed Young (above)
Book. Chinese Mother Goose Rhymes
The World Publishing Company

Artist. Etienne Delessert (right)
Book. Story Number 1
Harlin Quist Books

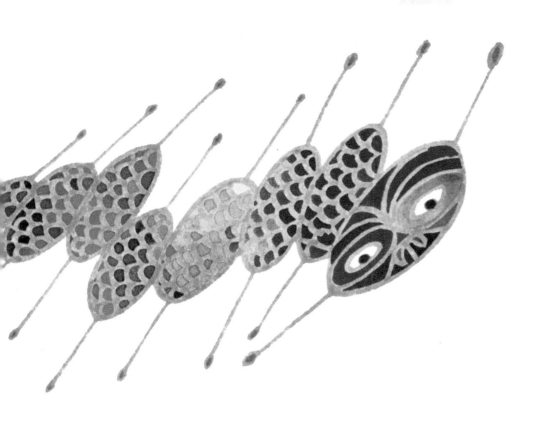

Artist. Jacob Lawrence (left)
Book. Harriet and the Promised Land
Simon & Schuster, Inc.

Artist. Uri Shulevitz (right)
Book. The Fool of the World and the Flying Ship
Farrar, Straus and Giroux

Artist. John Alcorn (below)
Book. Pocahontas in London
Delacorte Press

Artist. Nicole Clavelous (left)
Book. The Secret Journey of Hugo the Brat
Harlin Quist Books

Artist. Beni Montresor (right)
Book. I Saw a Ship A-Sailing
Alfred A. Knopf, Inc.

Artist. Lionel Kalish (below)
Book. The Cat and the Fiddler
Parents' Magazine Press

But the ladies and gentlemen of the court couldn't
stop dancing. Even the King himself couldn't stop dancing.
"Help! Help!" cried the King. "I'm tired.
Cat, stop your dancing. I command you. Stop!"
The cat, however, was not tired. She danced faster
and faster, and everyone else found themselves dancing
faster and faster. The cat danced outside the courtroom.
Everyone followed, dancing.
She danced down the palace steps.
Everyone followed, dancing.

Artist. Munro Leaf (left)
Book. I Hate You, I Hate You
Sterling Institute Press

Artist. Monica Alesci (above)
Book. I Belong
Herder and Herder

Artist. Ed Renfro (right)
Book. My Marvelous Menagerie
Holt, Rinehart & Winston, Inc.

TO A FAMILY.

15

If you would like a wonderful pet,
I'm sure you'd like my whale.
He cools me off on summer days;
Too bad — he's not for sale.

148

She scattered the demons to left and to right.

Hey and the rue grows bonnie wi' thyme

Artist. Evaline Ness (above)
Book. Kellyburn Braes
Holt, Rinehart & Winston, Inc.

Artists. Alice and Martin Provensen (left)
Book. Tales from the Ballet
Golden Press

Paperback Covers

Dust jackets were first wrapped around hard-cover books mainly to protect them and secondarily to advertise them. When the "paperback revolution" took place after World War II, soft-cover books began to appear on newsstands. But there they had to compete for attention with colorful and often gaudy magazine covers. So publishers called on artists to make paperback covers as striking, original and instantly informative as possible. The result has been a dazzling range of styles and approaches, all of them designed to make a potential customer stop and look, realize at once what the subject is—and buy the book.

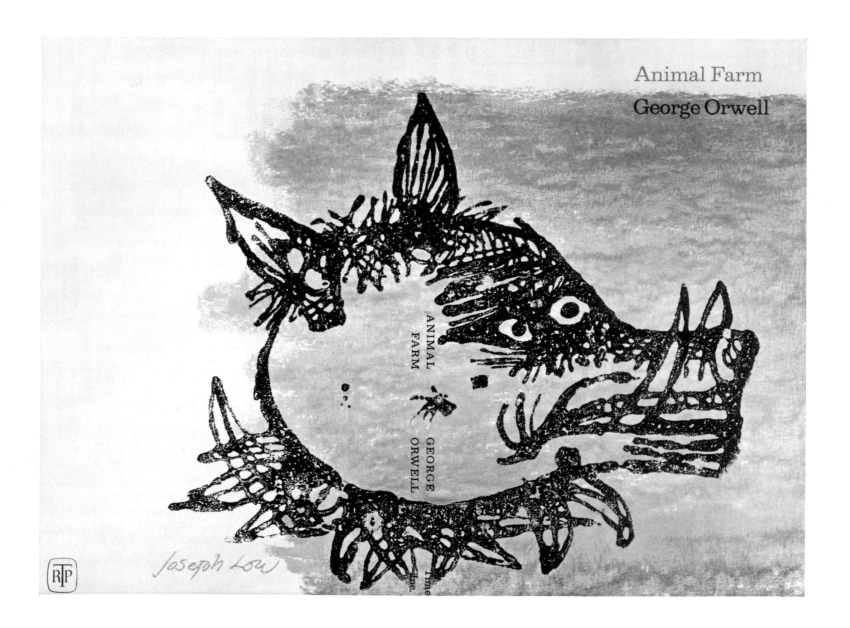

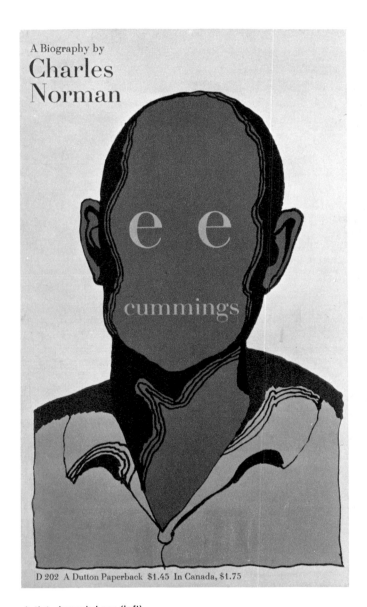

Artist. Joseph Low (left)
Art Director. Edward H. Hamilton
Book. Animal Farm
Time Inc.

Artist. Milton Glaser (above)
Book. e e cummings
E. P. Dutton & Co., Inc.

Artist. James McMullan (right)
Art Director. Cyril I. Nelson
Book. Modern Spanish Theatre
E. P. Dutton & Co., Inc.

Artist. Seymour Chwast (left)
Art Director. Harris Lewine
Book. The Bourgeois
Holt, Rinehart & Winston, Inc.

Artists. Scholl and Schneider
Book. Our Children's Burden
Random House, Inc.

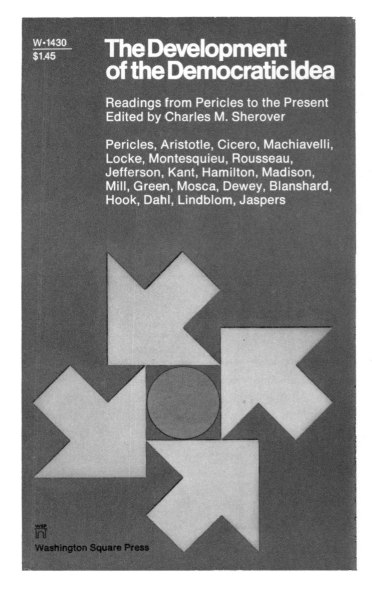

Artist. Robert Korn (left)
Art Director. Sol Immerman
Book. Compulsion and Doubt
Simon & Schuster, Inc.

Artist. John Haines
Art Director. Sol Immerman
Book. The Development of the Democratic Idea
Simon & Schuster, Inc.

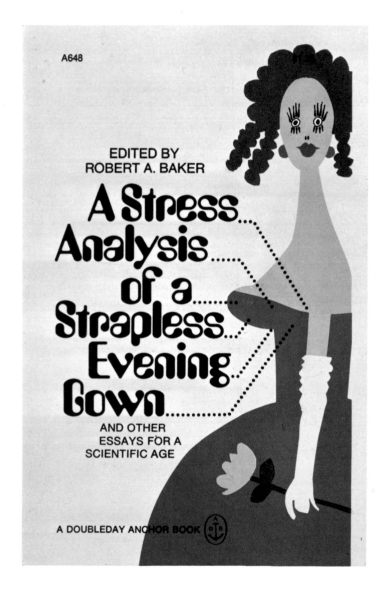

Artist. Kiyoshi Kanai (left)
Book. A Stress Analysis of a Strapless Evening Gown
Doubleday & Company, Inc.

Artist. Richard Milone
Book. Conjectures and Refutations: The Growth of
Scientific Knowledge
Harper & Row

Artist. Saul Lambert (left)
Art Director. Alex Gotfryd
Book. I, Lucifer
Doubleday & Company, Inc.

Artist. George Giusti (below left)
Book. Claudius the God
Random House, Inc.

Artist. Robert Jones
Book. Toulouse-Lautrec
Crowell-Collier and MacMillan Inc.

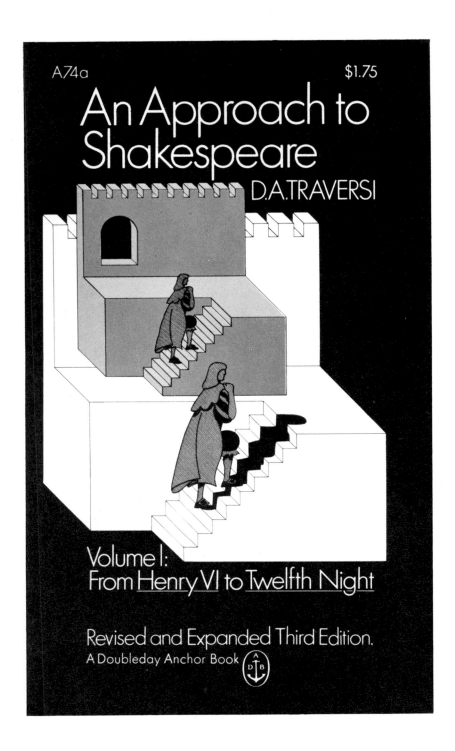

Artist. Kiyoshi Kanai (above)
Book. An Approach to Shakespeare
Doubleday & Company, Inc.

Artist. Emmanuel Schongut (right)
Book. The Odyssey of Homer
Harper & Row

Artist. Milton Charles (far right)
Art Director. Sol Immerman
Book. Euripides V
Simon & Schuster, Inc.

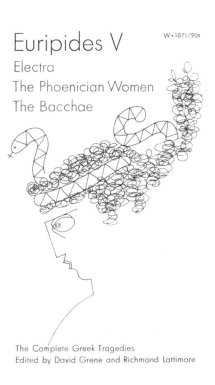

156

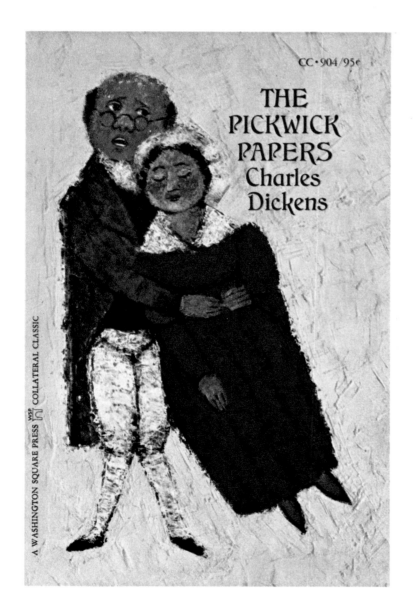

Artist. Milton Charles (left)
Art Director. Sol Immerman
Book. The Pickwick Papers
Simon & Schuster, Inc.

Artist. Eric von Schmidt (above)
Book. Notes of a Native Son
Bantam Books, Inc.

Record Album Covers

Obviously stimulated by the new music, from the Beatles to Baroque, the record companies have broken away from traditional romantic album covers and are trying stunning color, wild collages, and abstractions imposed on multiple exposures. Static art of the Beethoven bust variety is out, and striking graphics, neo-Art Nouveau and post-psychedelic designs are in. Although album covers are not a large field for an artist, they provide a widely distributed and prominent "showcase" for his work.

The Millenium Begin
Art Director/Designer. John Berg
Art. Geller & Butler Advertising
CBS Records

Ars Nova
Artist. Gene Szafran
Art Director/Designer. William S. Harvey
Elektra Records

RAMNAD KRISHNAN: *VIDWAN*

songs of the Carnatic tradition

Ramnad Krishnan, singer

V. Thyagarajan, violin

T. Ranganathan, mridangam

V. Nagarajan, kanjira

P. Srinivasan, tampura

Ramnad Krishnan: Vidwan
Artist. Robert Ziering
Art Director. William S. Harvey
Designer. Elaine Gongora
Nonesuch Records

The Wild Bull
Artist. Robert Pepper
Art Director. William S. Harvey
Designer. Elaine Gongora
Nonesuch Records

Earth Opera
Artist. Abe Gurvin
Art Director/Designer. William S. Harvey
Elektra Records

The Nonesuch Guide to Electronic Music
Artist. Gene Szafran
Art Director. William S. Harvey
Designer. Elaine Gongora
Nonesuch Records

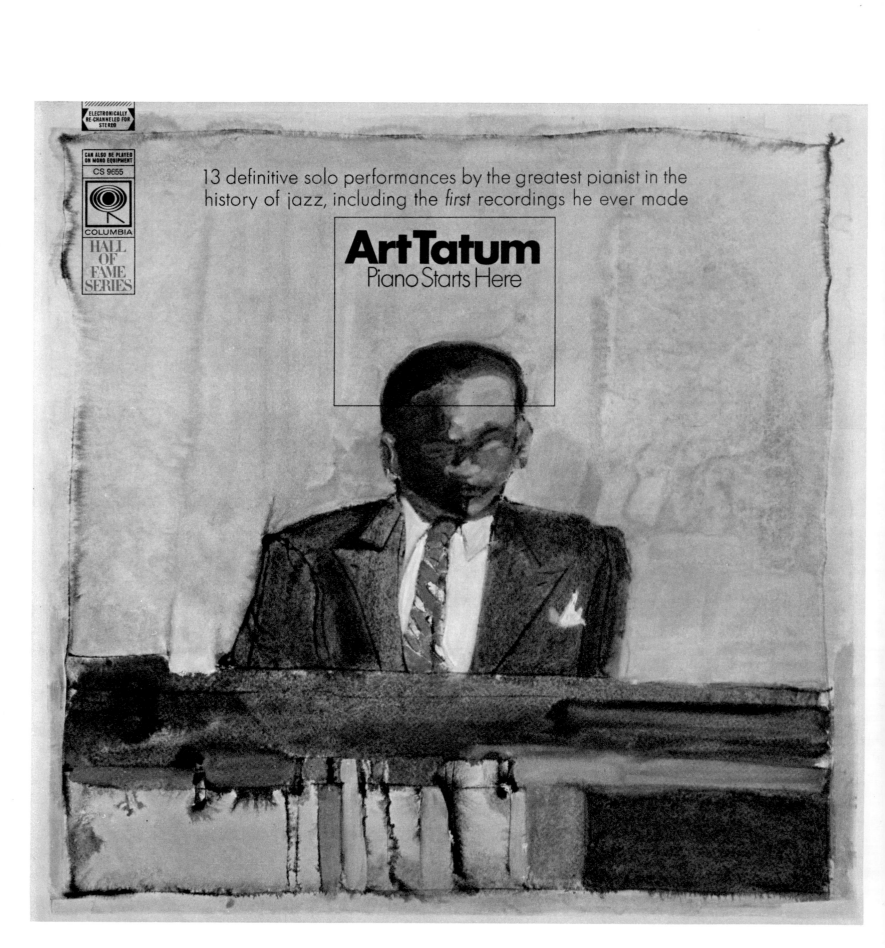

Art Tatum Piano Starts Here
Artist. Robert Andrew Parker
Art Director. John Berg
Designer. Henrietta Condak
CBS Records

Berlioz Symphonie Fantastique
Artist. Milton Glaser
Art Director/Designer. John Berg
CBS Records

The 12 London Symphonies
Artist. Abe Gurvin
Art Director. William S. Harvey
Designer. Elaine Gongora
Nonesuch Records

Six Artists Discuss Their Work

Six artists who are painters as well as illustrators discuss their recent work in a variety of fields. They have helped choose the works reproduced in these pages.

Ben Shahn

The artist. At the time of his death in 1969, Ben Shahn, long one of America's outstanding painters, was busy with some of the most ambitious projects of his career—as these pages attest. No follower of art fashions, he had gone his own way, a way not only of great personal integrity but one that enabled him to express himself both as an artist and as a thinking political being. Brought from Russia as a child, Shahn worked as a lithographer's apprentice while attending high school at night and later the National Academy of Design. Represented in almost every major museum in the United States, Shahn was the subject of several score articles and a number of books. He was for many years on the Guiding Faculty of Famous Artists School.

The artist speaks. During the 1920's I first realized that in order to express my own feelings and views in art, I could no longer try to paint in the style of Cézanne or Matisse or Picasso. I also became aware, through a deep questioning of my own beliefs, that I could no more follow my contemporaries on a road of increasing abstraction and disengagement than I could the traditional approaches. My background and experiences, as well as the Depression and then the war, had fostered in me a sharp political awareness and a strong sense of social justice.

I had always liked telling stories and in my travels back and forth across America I found I liked watching people— how they live, the individual qualities of each, the kinds of places they live in. In my painting now, I knew I had to express what I myself felt, that I had to paint the people and objects and situations before me as I found them— attentive to realistic detail, yes, but projected through my artist's inner eye. This way of thinking has dominated my art and is evident in two of my most recent works, the Sacco-Vanzetti mural that I did for Syracuse University in 1967 and a series of lithographs that I did for the poems of the German poet Rainer Maria Rilke.

One of Ben Shahn's twenty-eight lithographs illustrating Rilke's "Notebooks of Malte Laurids Brigge," a journal of a poet's impressions and dreams. The lithographs, Shahn says in his Afterword, were intended not to illustrate the text objectively but rather to express the emotions he experienced when he first read the book during a visit to Paris in 1927.

"I felt spiritually very close to this poet who had had many of the same experiences as I," Shahn writes. "Rilke's words touched me deeply. I, too, was just beginning to question my own innermost beliefs and to seek my own directions in art. Rilke's lines encouraged me to question, search, and doubt."

Shahn's Sacco and Vanzetti mural at Syracuse
(above, full view, and details at the right)

At the height of the national alarm over anarchistic
activities in the 1920's, Nicola Sacco and Bartolomeo
Vanzetti, two Italian immigrants in Boston, were
accused of the murder of a factory paymaster and
the robbery of $15,000. Despite numerous irregular-
ities in the case, they were convicted and sentenced
to death. Many Americans and Europeans thought
they had been put to death for their radical beliefs.

While Shahn was in Europe in 1925, he became aware
of the strong feelings the case had aroused, and on
his return to the United States, he threw himself into
the controversy. In 1930 he began a series of gouaches
about the trial, and two years later, when the Museum
of Modern Art was seeking mural sketches for future
commission, he entered a panel called "The Passion
of Sacco and Vanzetti." "For the first time," he says,
"I realized that the paint brush could evoke as great
a response as the fiery written word."

When in the fall of 1965 Syracuse University ap-
proached Shahn about doing a mural and said he
could use any subject, he thought immediately of his
Sacco and Vanzetti paintings. "Not only was this a
subject for public art," he writes, "but I was aware
that there was also a renewed interest in the controversy." He chose an outside wall of the Crouse
Building, making the doors at either end separate
the mural itself from the memorable statement made
by the poor shoemaker Vanzetti. Shahn thought the
mural was better integrated and stronger in compassionate feeling than his original painting.

Austin Briggs

The artist. During a long career as artist and illustrator Austin Briggs has won scores of awards from the Society of Illustrators, has explored every medium and many styles, and carried out a host of exciting assignments. The most interesting commissions in recent years have taken him to Viet Nam and into the troubled South, both for Look Magazine. Originally a Midwesterner, Briggs studied art in Detroit and in New York at the Art Students League and is one of the founders of the Famous Artists School. Some of the pieces from the notable collection of modern sculpture in his Connecticut home are reproduced elsewhere in these pages.

The artist speaks. Early in my career I chose to look for inspiration in museums and art galleries rather than in the work of other illustrators because I knew that what I could see in the museums was better. These artists worked from their own experience and feelings, to satisfy themselves, rather than on assignments to satisfy somebody else. I also decided that I would relate a part of my experience to every assignment I undertook. By "my experience" I mean all that I know and feel and comprehend of life.

A picture begins with a concept, and I can't say exactly how I arrive at any particular concept because each day I'm a different man. There are, however, certain procedures I almost always follow when I illustrate a manuscript. First, I read it as though I were looking at a movie, visualizing scenes, angles, characters. Next, I get as much information about the subject as I can. But one thing I don't want to know is anything other artists have already done on the same subject—anything that will interfere with my own point of view.

As I think about translating information into pictorial terms, I become involved. To help generate empathy, I think in such broad terms as love and hate, fear and courage. Then I work from these categories toward a concrete idea that will dramatize the generality. I strive for an interpretation that will bring out the extraordinary in the ordinary, and thus give impact to the picture, even though it may be only of a housewife in her kitchen, or a businessman in his office.

Somewhere in gathering information and in generating excitement, the picture concept begins to emerge. I begin to think of what Ben Shahn called "the shape of content," meaning the forms that most closely relate to the picture idea. For example, a picture of a mother and child calls for an expression of unity and containment that is effectively conveyed by an egg shape; a conflict, on the other hand, might take the form of shapes that act on each other with the clash and tensions best expressed by diagonals or jagged shapes.

The final decision pertains to medium. The medium that is right for one subject is not necessarily right for another. Watercolor is sparkling, spontaneous and lovely, but I probably wouldn't use it to make a powerful statement or create a solemn mood.

It isn't easy to analyze the creative process. But I can safely say that as long as I feel excited about what I'm doing, making an illustration is more than just carrying out an assignment. It is an opportunity to express myself, to work from my experience—to fulfill myself.

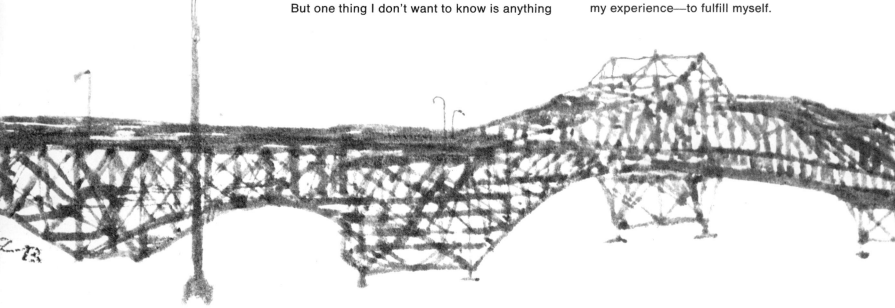

Above: Demonstrating the artist's striking range, this interpretation of a tropical reef glows with rich luminescent fish and fantastic vegetation. It was an unrestricted assignment from the Standard Oil Co. of New Jersey.

The bridge (below) and the tenement (right) are from a score of impressionistic sketches and paintings made by the artist for an issue on city problems in Lithopinion, the lively quarterly of graphic arts and current affairs of the Amalgamated Lithographers of America. Both pieces sensitively catch the signs of decay— the battered iron scrawl of an old bridge, and the corroded face of a slum façade.

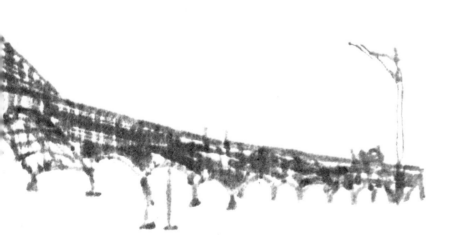

This poster was made for a movie on the St. Valentine's Day gangland massacre of the 1920's. The artist seeks to recapture the era with a collage of movie stills tied into a heart form that mocks the holiday of love.

Facing page, top: The style is relaxed but the interpretation is sharply focused in this illustration for a story in Ladies' Home Journal.

Center: A loose, richly atmospheric sketch made for a short story by Ray Bradbury in McCall's magazine.

Bottom: A cover for Status magazine sums up Victorian elegance, discreetly utilizing all the status symbols of the period.

Bernie Fuchs

The artist. In the sixteen years since Bernie Fuchs graduated from the Washington University School of Fine Arts in St. Louis, he has become one of the leading magazine illustrators, his work appearing regularly in McCall's, Look, Cosmopolitan and Sports Illustrated. Known for his magazine portrait illustration, he visits his subjects—including, for example, President John F. Kennedy and Dr. Martin Luther King— and photographs them as he talks to them. He lives in a rambling home in Westport, Connecticut, not far from the Famous Artists School, on whose Guiding Faculty he serves.

The artist speaks. The illustrations on these pages were done in a number of mediums, including photography. It may surprise some who are acquainted with my work that I should carry out an assignment with the camera rather than with pencil, pen or brushes, but I believe the medium is immaterial: what matter is using the means best suited to solving the problem.

The creative effort that went into the St. Valentine's Day Massacre illustration was no less ardent or arduous because the finished picture was made with a camera. It took a diligent hunt to find just the right setting, placement of figures, composition, interpretation of light, and point of view.

The great variety of publications and new communication techniques, and the tireless search for the unusual are some of the factors that are inviting artists to diversify their talents. I enjoy the challenge of communicating by various visual means and I'm glad that it's no longer necessary for an illustrator to restrict himself to the traditional graphic mediums, nor to remain categorized by art directors as a specialist in a certain style, subject, or technique.

An artist's most cherished objective is quality. It is important, therefore, that he exercise his eye and sensibilities to seek out the excellent in everything. The product of such self-cultivation is often called taste, and I believe that to be a successful artist one must cultivate a scale of values in which he believes and by which he can measure taste with assurance. His work will inevitably reflect his taste—and if the public accepts the work they will be accepting his taste, which is tantamount to considering it good.

George Giusti

The artist. George Giusti was born in Italy of Swiss and Italian parents and studied in Milan. He had a studio in Zurich before coming to the United States in 1938. Famous for striking designs that often make use of metal, wood, fabric and other materials as well as paint, he has won more than fifteen medals and eighty awards for his work. He has acted as art director of major campaigns for industrial companies and portfolios of his work have appeared in all the leading art magazines of the world. He is a member of the Founding Faculty of Famous Artists School.

The artist speaks. I believe that every true artist is a discoverer, forever seeking new horizons to explore. His is a continual search for clues that help him envision the world of tomorrow. He looks upon accepted forms and conventions, not as immutable laws but as forerunners of new concepts and solutions. He is a free man, and is not ruled by false notions of what must be and what must not be.

The timid artist barricades himself behind a wall of the familiar and banal; over his gate he has written: "Let nothing new enter here!" At the other extreme is the immoderate artist who pursues the unconventional for its own sake. In art, as in society, to make a cult of chaos is to be negative and destructive.

The true artist delves deeply into his own fantasies. But he is no idle dreamer; his feet are on firm ground. The unconscious is a bottomless reservoir from which he draws the raw material for his creativity. With his conscious mind he takes the nebulous and translates it into logical and useful concepts. Thus he turns dreams into reality and relates them to the present. It is impossible to be creative without this interchange between fantasy and the real. To dream is natural, but it takes work, and more work, to mold vague ideas into an art and a reality that is far above and beyond the easy alternatives of the past or present.

HOLIDAY

JULY 1968 – 75c

MEXICO
A SPECIAL ISSUE

Far left: A bold simple image makes an arresting cover for a Mexico issue of Holiday

Above: The artist used polished brass in this modern interpretation of the knight-in-armor trademark of the Champion Paper Company.

Left: For a Command Records album called "Brass Impact" the artist created a brass-sheet sculpture that both focuses attention and states the theme.

Lorraine Fox

The artist. An exponent of decorative design with a leaning toward the primitive, Lorraine Fox has ranged from painting to advertising and editorial art, book illustration, and the design of wallpaper and fabrics. A graduate of Pratt Institute who also studied with Reuben Tam at the Brooklyn Museum Art School, she teaches illustration at Parsons and is now on the Guiding Faculty of the Famous Artists School. She lives with her husband, the illustrator Bernard D'Andrea, in Great Neck on Long Island.

The artist speaks. What is important is how much an artist grows as an individual, and how personal his statement continues to be, not how excellent he becomes technically—although this may follow. The creative part is the very personal statement that leads to original concepts, which in turn must lead to a more individual statement in drawing, design, color, and finally in technique.

An artist often shifts his approach, depending on how restless he is. Some artists feel it is important to try a new technique for each job. Other artists may seem to the outsider to change very little, but to themselves the change may be quite obvious.

Over the years, I have passed through many approaches to my work, seeking what I feel I can do best. I rarely remain with one approach for very long—although commercial art almost forces one to do this—because there is always the danger of falling into a rut. I change my approach often to prevent boredom and maintain freshness.

I think these comments apply to all committed artists, whether they are commercial or fine artists. However, I do make a distinction between the two: the fine artist works entirely from within, not just for the sake of originality but to achieve self-realization through a unique way of seeing. A dedicated artist will retain this point of view whether it is saleable or not.

The problems faced by an illustrator who is trying to win respect as a commercial artist are quite different. As in all art, if he is to hold his own in his field, his approach must remain flexible. It is a rare artist who is so unique as to be able to use only one approach and have it appreciated over a long period of time.

Sometimes my procedure is to work out an illustration beforehand; at other times I may let it evolve as I work. Then again, I may work out the whole piece straightaway. All this depends on my mood or the specifications of the job.

As for my paintings, they do not evolve from any specific external stimulus but from an inner vision, one which I may have been turning over for many years. In commercial assignments, whether it be a manuscript, an "on the spot" drawing, or even a free choice, I am still limited by preconceived subject matter that someone else plans to use in mass communications media. For me this is the vital difference between doing an illustration and a painting.

One's ideas for paintings may not be so original at the beginning, but in the course of time a distillation takes place and they become more purely one's own. There has been a carry-over of this development into my commercial work in recent years. My new illustrations are becoming more personal and more conceptual. By conceptual I mean an intellectual solution for an assignment rather than a purely retinal one. Fortunately, due to the influence of the many new approaches to fine art, the illustrator need not be content with a purely retinal picture.

Far left: A cell-like image for a story in Seventeen Magazine is made to represent the plight of a white girl and a black girl who are roommates at college.

Right above: This greeting card for American Artists Group is a rich concentration of old-fashioned objects and folk motifs.

Right: An illustration for Somebody Came, a children's book by Mark Van Doren (Harlin Quist Books), emphasizes the smallness of a house in which a little girl and her grandfather live.

Syd Solomon

The artist. Syd Solomon was born in Union-town, Pennsylvania, studied in Paris at the Ecole des Beaux Arts and at the Chicago Art Institute. Although his forms are abstract he uses vivid color to express his delight in the natural world. A zestful man who likes the outdoors, he spends his summers at East Hampton, L. I., and his winters on the west coast of Florida. He has taught in various art schools and is on the Guiding Faculty of Famous Artists School. He is represented in the Baltimore Museum of Art, the Whitney Museum of American Art and a score of other museums.

The artist speaks. My beginning ideas for a painting are connected with that exuberant feeling of flux that has been my starting point for many years. The distillations of this process produce the abstractions and simplifications of "reality" that I am looking for.

My preliminary paintings in watercolor or gouache often open up to me a fresh sense of pictorial space, for they are frequently swift excursions into pure light—a shorthand report of a new experience. The interaction between materials and ideas intrigues me, and has prompted my adventures into experimental mediums. The unknown effects—accidents, if you wish—of mixed media and new techniques awakens responses in me that are plastically useful. They arouse visual memories that might otherwise remain neglected. How valid these unknowns prove is the painter's problem; it is up to me to fit them into a framework of directed effort and previous experience.

Contemporary trends are a constant reminder to me that discovery is vital to art. Even if I am not convinced of the importance of the collective trends, I do find that the ideas of a few brilliant young men excite me by confirming my own changes and my own searchings.

For the new building of the St. Petersburg Times, the artist painted a heroic mural (8′ x 13′), called "Suncoast," that fuses land, sea and sky as well as docks and ports of Florida's West Coast into a sparkling, airy abstraction.

Right: "Cameo for Giotto," paying homage to the Old Master in the shape of a pendent, translates the forms and colors of Giotto into contemporary visual terms.

Left: All the artist's feeling for the sand, surf, light, dunes and tidepools near his East Hampton studio are blended in this painting called "Polyscape."

The Artist in the Theater

by Shareen Blair

Helium-filled silver pillows dangle, dance and float offstage into the audience. Movies and slide projections flicker over the dancers. Activated by the passage of a dancer through its electronic field, a series of radio antennae becomes a set of sounds. Scenic design, once the passive, retiring handmaiden of opera, dance and drama, has embraced the kinetic strivings of the art of the Sixties. It is no longer easy to distinguish between a set and a happening, a painting and a performance.

Theater design has again become the legitimate province of the painter and sculptor. The association of painters Robert Rauschenberg, Jasper Johns, Andy Warhol and Frank Stella and film-maker Stan VanDerBeek with choreographer Merce Cunningham, during his recent seasons at the Brooklyn Academy of Music, testifies to the inspiration artists are finding in the theater. Involvement in the performing arts means freedom for the artist both from the physical isolation of his studio and the two-dimensional restrictions of a canvas. It also means exposure to a larger audience than he has in a gallery show. A few painters, notably Robert Whitman and Warhol, have found the theater and film environment so stimulating that they have temporarily abandoned painting.

The Influence of Diaghilev

It was Serge Diaghilev, the Russian impresario, who inspired the original movement from the painter's studio to the stage. Beginning in St. Petersburg during the 1890's, he gathered a group of painters, composers, choreographers and librettists, and during the next three decades they collaborated in the production of extraordinarily successful ballets and operas.

Set design before Diaghilev had lagged far behind the artistic movements of the day. The designing of a theatrical production was left to the discretion of the carpenter, scene-painter, dressmaker and, worse yet, the performer. To achieve his scenic goals—the simplification of stage décor by the elimination of realistic details (painted wooden trees, papier-mâché rocks),

the abolition of the perspective backcloth, and the harmonious coordination of both costume and scenery—Diaghilev commissioned the leading artists of his day. Pablo Picasso, André Derain, Juan Gris, Georges Braque, Joan Miró, Naum Gabo, Georgio de Chirico and Georges Rouault were some who provided sets and costumes for Diaghilev's Ballets Russes.

The majority of Diaghilev's artists viewed the stage as one vast moving canvas. Although Diaghilev's objective was a theater where dance, music and design were completely blended, in the later years of the company's existence the painter's vision frequently overpowered the production in a profusion of line and color.

The Sculptor as Designer

Another solution to the problem of designing a set was proposed by two influential designers, the Englishman Gordon Craig and the Swiss Adolphe Appia. Their approach was primarily sculptural and their sets for operas and plays, composed of minimal symbolic forms, relied upon specially developed lighting techniques. The suggestive use of sculptural forms has perhaps been most successfully exploited by Isamu Noguchi. His sets for the Martha Graham Company and the New York City Ballet rely upon elementary symbolism of form to suggest the entire theme of a dance. The Noguchi-Graham collaboration has been a remarkable one. Often the set—for example, the triptych designed for "Seraphic Dialogue"—is integrated into the dance movement itself.

Breaking through the Stage Frame

Whether it is conceived as an animated canvas or a sculptural construction, traditionally the function of scenery was the creation of an environment, an illusion of reality. During the 1930's and early 1940's while figurative painting still dominated the art scene, set design continued to be more or less related to easel painting. After the war, the Abstract Expressionists or Action painters, shifting the focus from the object painted to the act of painting, created new conditions for art. Painters, preoccupied with the new problems of tensions and the fluidity of space, created larger, more monumental canvases. Abstract or non-thematic dance was also in vogue, and set design responded to this stimulus, too. Stage space opened up. The stark, blue backdrop, the cyclorama, was used to suggest the wide-open out-of-doors.

The theory developed by the Action painters that a painting is essentially fragmentary and larger than its boundaries is related to the theatrical idea that neither the set nor the proscenium stage need restrict a performance spatially. Now, the boundary between art and life has become so thin that often actors, musicians and dancers mingle and interact with the audience. In "Astarte," a collaboration between choreographer Robert Joffrey and lighting designer Tom Skelton, the dance begins with a man in street clothes who walks through the audience onto the stage, undresses and dances with a girl amidst such multimedia as strobe lighting, stereophonic sound effects, and movies playing over the dancers and against the sets. The dance has no true climax but simply terminates when the man exits out onto the street.

The Cunningham Revolution

This kind of theater where art has some of the accidental quality of life is also indebted to the Pop artists. By taking objects from their everyday surroundings and thrusting them into a theatrical context, the Pop artists broke down old patterns of seeing, inviting the public to view their environment with fresh eyes. Rauschenberg, in a piece entitled "Story," designed for the Cunningham company, introduced chance into the make-up of the set, which changed radically with each new theater that housed it. The entire backstage area was opened up and such objects as tires, step-ladders, ironing-boards collected in a pre-performance scavenger hunt, provided the décor. Dancers were permitted to wear costumes selected from a pile ranging from Salvation Army leftovers to strings of plastic bottles and football shoulder pads.

Cunningham's collaborators have effected another revolution: instead of leaving the stage clear for the dancers, they often furnish it with lifelike obstructions. Dancers must work around Stella's aluminum-suspended banners or Johns' vinyl boxes much as pedestrians must negotiate sidewalks filled with fire-hydrants, lamp posts and trash baskets.

Although the dance has, in this century, been the most prominent patron of the artist, drama directors here and abroad have turned to artists to design for them. David Hockney provided sets for London's Royal Court Theater production of "Ubu Roi" by Alfred Jarry. Jim Dine introduced many elements (saws, hammers, pots and pans) from his paintings into his designs for the San Francisco Workshop's staging of Shakespeare's "A Midsummer Night's Dream."

Set design changes as new theater forms emerge. Off-Broadway performances have been inundated with new techniques—cinematic projections ("Your Own Thing"), photographs of sets masquerading as the real thing ("The Boys in the Band"), psychedelic, glow-in-the-dark colors, and strobe lighting effects ("Hair") —borrowed from the galleries and discotheques.

The need many people feel for visual stimulation is perhaps most readily satisfied by the opera and musical comedy. Marc Chagall, Beni Montresor, Ming Cho Lee and Rouben Ter-Arutunian are among the prominent artists working in these media. The challenge of modern opera has prompted one company, the Minneapolis Center Opera, to employ an avant-garde artist, Robert Indiana, to do the sets for Virgil Thompson's "The Mother of Us All."

Invaded by new refinements in technology— revolving and thrust stages, automated lighting equipment—the theater has greatly expanded its range of expression and consequently also its dependence on the engineer and lighting technician. New materials—steel and aluminum tubing, polystyrene, plexiglass—inspire new scenic solutions. The only limit to the visual revolution within the theater is the imagination of the artist and the spectator.

Isamu Noguchi: for "Seraphic Dialogue"
Martha Graham Dance Company
This stark set, a sculptural adaptation of a
medieval painted triptych, suggests the religious nature of the subject—Joan of Arc.

Jasper Johns: for "Walkaround Time"
Merce Cunningham Dance Company
For this magical set, Johns borrowed motifs—
a chocolate grinder, cones, etc.—from "The
Large Glass" by the Dadaist master, Marcel
Duchamp. He then silk-screened the images
upon transparent vinyl boxes.

184

Marc Chagall: for "The Firebird" (left)
Curtain designed for the American Ballet
Theater production, later adapted by the
New York City Ballet
Of Chagall's many designs for the theater,
including the present production of "The Magic
Flute" for the Metropolitan Opera, it is the
"Firebird" set, perhaps because of the Russian
idiom, which best complements the choreog-
raphy (by Balanchine) and the music (by
Stravinsky).

Pablo Picasso: for "Le Tricorne" (The Three-
Cornered Hat) (left below)
Sketch for the Diaghilev Ballets Russes
production
For this ballet, based on Spanish themes,
Picasso not only painted much of the decor
but also supervised the design of the props
and costumes and the facial makeup of the
performers.

David Hockney: for "Ubu Roi" (right)
Sketches for two scenes
In his designs for Alfred Jarry's play, the
English Pop artist used Jarry's own drawings
and directions as a source of inspiration.

Robert Rauschenberg: for "Summerspace"
The New York City Ballet production of the
Merce Cunningham work
The pointillist dots of the costumes and backdrop as they merge, creating the effect
of a large moving canvas, recall the paintings
of Seurat.

Alex Katz: for "Junction"
The Paul Taylor Dance Company
Paul Taylor is another modern dance choreographer who has turned to avant-garde painters,
among them Katz and Ellsworth Kelly, for
décor and costumes.

Jim Dine: for "A Midsummer Night's Dream"
San Francisco Actor's Workshop
In this costume sketch, Dine has provided
Shakespeare's character, Peter Quince, a carpenter, with the tools of his trade. The actual
costumes derived much of their effect from
Dine's emphasis on contrasting textures—
rough burlap, leopard-skin, Naugahyde, army
camouflage, satins and silver lamé.

Cecil Beaton: for "My Fair Lady"
Costume sketch
Among the most prominent of the British
designers working in the theater, Beaton's
costumes for the Ascot Race sequence of
"My Fair Lady," using only black and white,
set a new standard for elegance in the
musical theater.

4 The Great Traditions

Old Masters and New Magic

by Nancy Kaufman

Van Gogh-Delacroix
During his confinement in the asylum at
St. Rémy, the emotionally distraught Vincent
Van Gogh began copying paintings as a kind
of therapy. "Since I have no models," he
wrote, "I use the black-and-whites by Delacroix and Millet... as I would a real-life subject."
Copying from a monochrome reproduction,
Van Gogh invented his own color scheme, and
this, along with his serpentine line and paint-
thick brush strokes, make the style entirely
his own.

Part of the twentieth century rebellion against
tradition has been a turning away from the
systematic emulation of the old masters. As far
back as 1919, Marcel Duchamp, one of the
"enfants terribles" of modern art, expressed
this attitude when he painted Mona Lisa with a
moustache and goatee. Other modern painters
have parodied the classics or done new versions bringing old themes up to date.

Does this signify a disrespect for the great of
the past? Hardly. It is simply a declaration of
independence. We will study and learn from the
old masterpieces as we please, the modern
painter says, but we will not ape them or follow
their lead. So we should not be altogether surprised when an avant-garde American painter,
Larry Rivers, declares in an interview: "Old
masters are my favorite painters. I have no illusion as to their influence on my work."

Looking closely, we find that many modern
artists have used an old painting as a starting
point for a work of their own. Picasso, for
example, seems to be constantly challenged by
the works of certain masters and is forever
finding new interpretations for them. In some
instances, such as Velasquez's "Las Meninas"
and Delacroix's "Woman of Algiers," he virtually
exhausted the compositional and stylistic possibilities of each painting by making dozens of
studies of it.

Whatever the reason that an artist uses a particular work—whether to learn from it, to rein-
terpret it, to parody the conventions of an
earlier age or to satirize the values of his own
time—he will, if he is successful, make it
uniquely his own. When we see the two side-by-
side we find that the modern version gives new
meaning to the old master, revealing both the
strength and weakness of the new and the old.

Each artist is a master of his art and each
speaks for his own time. The modern painting is
an entirely new and independent work of art. It is
then paying homage to the original, accepting
the earlier work not as a painting but as a living
experience with the power to stimulate that a
great experience has in the life of any artist.

Levine-Titian
Jack Levine recalls Titian's "Rape of Europa" fondly, having seen it often in the Gardner Museum in his native Boston. In his parody, "Titian Misremembered," made years later, Levine converts the awesome episode of godly violence into a homely scene of play. A doll-like Europa seems pleased at being abducted, and the fierce bull-god becomes a tame creature quite undisturbed by the uproar he has set off among Europa's abandoned companions.

Matisse-de Heem
While he was still interested in the Cubist approach,
Matisse turned to Jan David de Heem's "Still Life,"
and in "La Dessert" converted it into a geometric
pattern. In a sense, he carried the already well-
defined planes, typical of Dutch still lifes and interiors,
to a logical Cubist conclusion.

Miró-Steen
Charmed by old Dutch genre paintings during a trip to Holland, Joan Miró later reworked several of them. In "Dutch Interiors II" (1928), inspired by Jan Steen's "The Cat's Dancing Lesson," the face of the bearded man becomes a spider, the vase, towel and table shrink to miniatures, and the jolly revelers become amorphous creatures revolving in gravity-less space. The original elements are still present but magically transformed into Miró's unique vocabulary of dream and fantasy.

Picasso-Courbet
The Cubists saw Courbet as the first to define
the density of the objects he painted, as in
"Demoiselles au bord de la Seine" (1856), where
the two women merge in one rocklike unit.
In Picasso's version all other elements—foliage,
sky, boat – are blended into this central from.

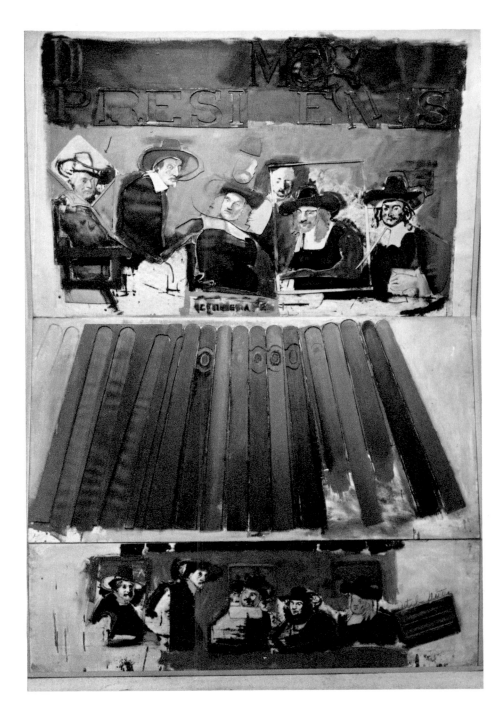

Rivers-Rembrandt

Out of a profound admiration of great paintings,
Larry Rivers in his "Dutch Masters" points up
the irony by which Rembrandt's "Syndics"
becomes the advertising symbol of a cigar.

Dali-Vermeer

Salvador Dali recalls that whenever he saw the copy of Vermeer's "The Lacemaker" in his father's study, he thought of rhinoceros horns. Thus, when he began to sketch it in the 1950's, the first thing that appeared on his pad was a horn, and he was convinced that rhino horns, forming a "perfect logarithmic spiral," had also guided Vermeer's hand. Although the exploding horns almost dominate Dali's version, the original painting, caught in glowing highlights that echo Vermeer's ethereal light, is still miraculously present.

The Innocent Eye: Naive Art

by Owen Rachleff

With the increasing complexities of the modern world and the sophistication of modern art, there is a certain pleasure in being able to turn from time to time to what is called naive or primitive painting. In the work, for example, of Rousseau, Kane, Bombois, Hicks, Pippin and Grandma Moses, in the "limners" of early America, and in some European folk artists there is a freshness, a simplicity, an innocence that beguiles and charms, that leads us back into a time and a world with which we have, unfortunately, lost touch.

Such art is a refuge from chaos, an escape if you wish, but what law says that a painting must be a reflection of the disorder of our time or of the bitterness of the artist? Must art be so artful or subtle or cryptic or noncommunicative that no one is sure what it is or whether it will still be interesting to anybody once the novelty or shock wears off?

It is not easy to say what naive art is as compared with the work of the trained artist, but that is a problem for critics, and it need not interfere with our appreciation of the naive. In general, a naive painting is the work of someone who has not studied the art of the past or has for some reason remained uninfluenced by it. The naive artist is generally literal even when he is painting, as Rousseau often did, a dream. Compared with that of the schooled artist, his work may appear to be crude or quaint. When it is poor it is only crude or quaint, but in the most successful work its crudeness will give it force and strength, its quaintness will strike us as fresh and original. And it may be childlike but it will not seem childish; that is, it will view the world with the child's wide-eyed innocence and wonder but with the completeness of vision that only a mature artist has.

There are other qualities that distinguish the naive artist. Unlike the schooled artist he is by nature not interested in how anyone else paints or in devices for creating illusions. He may not be accurate in his treatment of perspective or the relative size of objects but he makes up for

this in the way he magnifies details that a sophisticated painter would disdain or neglect. In other words, his innocence—even his ignorance—may be a virtue in a world where so many trained painters have lost the capacity to see with the innocent eye.

One result of this is that the naive artist's style rarely develops or undergoes any significant changes. A naive artist may even be quite incapable of change, unable to see a country scene, a sitter, a flower or an interior in any other way but as he has always seen it. Snowscapes from the early as well as the late paintings of Grandma Moses show the same stark white, chalky scene. When friends suggested that she give depth to the snow by adding blue shadows in the manner of Pissarro or Monet, Mrs. Moses threw up her hands and exclaimed: "I have looked at the snow and looked at the snow and I can see no blue."

This is interesting because we tend to think of naive artists as trying to be true to nature and as painting exactly what is in front of them. But such "children of nature" do not paint what they see but what they think they see. Grandma Moses looked at snow that had depth and was not always chalky white but she did not know how to convey that depth and she did not realize that the snow was not always chalky white. But at the same time, because of her lack of training she had a way of seeing that was entirely her own, with a sense of detail and color and composition that was, at its best, charming and warm.

Because a good naive artist has not been exposed to long and rigorous training, he will run less risk of seeming derivative or imitative. He will choose subjects he knows deeply and likes, and no second-hand notions of how he should paint will get between him and his subject. We are talking of course only of the good naive artist; the inferior primitive will have all the faults of any inferior painting and a few others that only a painter that lacks training as well as talent will have.

The naive artist is also almost never affected by trends in art or the way the world is going. As a consequence he will not relate to his period or his contemporaries. He may in fact show more of a kinship with naive artists of other lands and other periods. Certainly a mid-nineteenth century American primitive painter like Edward Hicks has more in common with an early twentieth century American artist like Pippin than he does with his academic contemporaries. If you like such art you may say that it is timeless and universal; if you are unsympathetic to it, you may feel that it is monotonous and limited.

Though he cannot be developed by training, the naive artist is perennial. He continues to crop up everywhere, especially among the "masses" and in the emerging cultures of Africa and South America. Even the complexities of modern life and the bombardment of the "media explosion" do not seem to affect the essentially innocent and uncomplicated image of naive art.

That is all to the good, for the optimism of the naive artist, his freshness and his desire to present things without puzzles or problems has genuine significance in the current struggle for social identity.

Henri Rousseau (above).
The Dream.
A minor French customs official,
Rousseau was known as Le Douanier.
Collection Museum of Modern Art, New York

Horrace Pippin (left).
Domino Players.
An American Negro, Pippin worked on a
farm, in a coal yard and as a hotel porter.
The Phillips Collection, Washington, D.C.

Grandma Moses (left above).
Sugaring Off.
The wife of an upstate New York
farmer, Anna Mary began to paint regularly
at the age of sixty-seven and produced
thousands of paintings before death at
the age of 101.
Grandma Moses Properties, Inc.

Morris Hirschfield (left).
Nude at Window.
M. Martin Janis Collection

Raphael Gonzalez y Gonzalez (right).
El Incendio del Volcan de San Pedro
La Laguna.
A Guatemalan, Gonzalez taught school in
his native town of San Pedro La Laguna
for eleven years before dedicating himself
to painting.
Museum of Natural History, Guatemala.

EL INCENDIO DEL
VOLCAN DE
SAN PEDRO L L.
Raf. Gonzalez G.

A. C. Slingerland (left). The Roman Catholic
Church of Zoeterwoude in 1900.
Born in Holland, Slingerland was a farmer.
Albert Dorne Collection of Naive Art

Ludmila Prochazkova (below).
Wedding-Party.
This scene was painted by a
Czechoslovak housewife.
Albert Dorne Collection of Naive Art

Streeter Blair (right). The Eisenhower Farm, Gettysburg, Pa. Blair was a Kansas highschool teacher and antiques dealer. Collection Sari Heller Gallery, Beverly Hills. Photo Galerie St. Etienne, New York

Ivan Lackovic (below). Village in Winter. A Yugoslav born in Croatia, Lackovic was a farmer and laborer. Photo Galerie St. Etienne

Ilija Bosilj (left). Village of Christ.
Bosilj was a Yugoslav farmer.
Albert Dorne Collection of Naive Art

Thea Gerard (right). My sister.
The artist was a Dutch housewife.
Albert Dorne Collection of Naive Art

Stjepan Vecenaj (right below).
The Shepherd's Dream.
Vecenaj, a farmer, was born in Gola,
Yugoslavia.
Galerie St. Etienne

Joseph Victor Gatto (above).
Times Square at Night.
Born in Greenwich Village, New York,
Gatto was a professional fighter, plumber's
assistant and a steamfitter.
Roy Neuberger Collection

Bill Maynard (left above). My Army Camp.
Maynard, a young Englishman born in
Newbury, Berkshire, left college and
worked until recently as an itinerant
gardener.
Portal Gallery, London

Mawasi Ram (left). Untitled.
Born in a village near Delhi, India, Ram
sold clay until his talent was discovered.
Gallery Konarak, New Delhi

The Persistence of Dada and Surrealism

by Wallace Brockway

Around the turn of the century, many young artists grew tired of Impressionism, the exhaustive study of light and form that had occupied such very different painters as Claude Monet and Paul Cézanne. The rebels had ideas of their own and could even refer to Cézanne's lovingly painted still-lifes as his "old apples." Art revolutions came on explosively: fauvism, the ism of the "wild beasts," with no program except a wild exaltation of color; and Cubism, in which objects were analyzed and reconstructed in geometric shapes. After that there was Futurism, which tried to animate Cubism and suggest the dynamism of the modern age. The Futurists defined beauty as the speed of a motor car, not as a Greek statue. They spoke of a new space, declaring that "henceforth the spectator would be placed in the heart of the picture."

Each movement revamped traditional art forms to keep pace with a society advancing into the age of technology. But the bright promise of the new age was quickly tarnished by the greatest war the world had yet seen. It was plain that scientific and technological advances could as easily dehumanize and destroy man as serve him. Against such a threat, the old forms and old ideas were plainly inadequate. So it was that Dada came about.

The Dada Outburst

Dada (a word that means "hobbyhorse" in French but was chosen at random) was a concerted movement in all the arts. Yet it was also much more. It was a revolution, and its effects are still being felt. As Tristan Tzara put it, "There is a great negative work of destruction to be accomplished. We must sweep and clean. Affirm the cleanliness of the individual after the madness of a world abandoned to bandits who rend one another and destroy the centuries . . . Dada; abolition of memory: Dada; abolition of archeology: Dada; abolition of prophets: Dada; abolition of the future: Dada; absolute . . . faith in every god that is the immediate product of spontaneity. . . . Freedom: Dada Dada Dada . . . an interlacing of all contradictions, grotesques, inconsistencies: LIFE."

Dada appeared in the middle of World War I, and its first aim was to annihilate standards in art and, even more startling, the very class, the bourgeoisie, in which such standards flourished. So a frenzied task force of artists, writers and musicians converged on Zurich, in neutral Switzerland, in 1916, and assailed the world in a series of uninhibited oral and visual exhibitions. They attacked the established order with mad recitations, bizarre visual constructions, and jarring music. The highly respectable citizens of Zurich were scandalized and the police soon closed the Dadaist meeting places and exhibitions.

Chance and the Unconscious

Among the most inventive creators of the new visual explosions was Hans Arp. His colored papers, woodcuts and sculptures were organized as free forms—"free" because created, he said, by chance. "The law of chance, which embraces all laws . . ." he wrote, "can only be experienced through complete devotion to the unconscious." At the same time, Francis Picabia painted functionless machines to satirize the science that had served the war. And the spirit behind all of this calculated "nonsense" was logical, witty Marcel Duchamp. Among his contributions were the notorious "ready-mades," existing objects that could be decorated or profaned according to whim, such as a print of the "Mona Lisa," to which he added a moustache, or a snow shovel that could simply be signed and called art.

Dada shattered all definitions of art. The important thing about Dada, Jean Arp said, "is that the Dadaists despised what is commonly regarded as art, but put the whole universe on the lofty throne of art. We declared that everything that comes into being or is made by man is art. Art can be evil, boring, wild, sweet, dangerous, ugly, or a feast to the eyes. The whole earth is art. . . . The nightingale is a great artist. Michelangelo's 'Moses': Bravo! But at the sight of an inspired snowman, the Dadaists also cry bravo."

René Magritte. Personal Values (1952).
Collection Harry Torczyner, New York.
Belgian artist Magritte assembles the
commonplaces of everyday life, but detached
from reality and blown up monstrously into a
surreal unity.

Man Ray. The Gift (c. 1958. Replica by the artist
after the original of 1921).
Collection the Museum of Modern Art,
New York.
This American artist and photographer
mocks bourgeois forms by putting a row of
tacks along the bottom of a flatiron.

Ancestors

Dada as a cry of anguished negation was dying as the war ended. But it had cleared the way for almost anything to happen in art. The first post-Dada outgrowth of Dadaism was Surrealism—a movement devoted to expressing man's unconscious. Dada alone did not produce Surrealism. The Surrealist impulse—dissatisfaction with reality and a taste for the paradoxical, the illogical, the mysterious—had a long ancestry of drawings, paintings and even sculpture—works that abolished the boundaries between the "real" and the "unreal." Hieronymus Bosch, the great Flemish painter whose fantastic "Garden of Delights" (1500) is a shifting world of reality and nightmares, was one of the Surrealist ancestors. The terrifying "Caprichos" (1799) of that Spanish genius, Francisco Goya, suggested that truth can be found only in the unreal. Even traditional works sometimes have had surreal overtones.

Odilon Redon, a Frenchman who died just when Dada was making its appearance, was another Surrealist ancestor. He considered himself a Surrealist, though he never used the term. At least one of his "axioms" is completely Surrealist: "All is done by docile submission to the uprush of the unconscious." And a critic wrote of him: "When Redon paints a girl or a flower, the girl is almost a flower, and the flower almost a girl"—an allusion to the shapeshifting that occurs in dreams.

Giorgio de Chirico, an Italian born in Greece, introduced an element of hallucination that many Surrealists were to borrow. According to Chirico, "a work of art must go far beyond the limits of man. Good sense and logic have no place in it. This is how a painting can approximate a dreamlike work of art." This is sound Surrealist doctrine. Chirico's landscapes flout the rules of perspective, light and shadow; and an enigmatic horror broods over them. His best work, certainly Surrealist, was done before the early 1920's.

In the Light of Freud

Surrealism, quite apart from its antecedents in art (and apart from Dada), owed much to Freud. Even before the 1920's Freud was becoming influential, particularly through his exploration of sex, dreams and the unconscious. His assertion that the child and the savage—and the artist—are in close touch with the liberated unconscious greatly influenced the Surrealists who said that reason—"good sense and logic" —had nothing to do with art. And Salvador Dali was to use Freud's writings almost as textbooks in recording psychiatric states in his pictures.

Surrealism was in the making even before Dada broke up. Max Ernst, the "complete Surrealist artist," was painting Surrealist pictures long before the movement was officially launched in 1924. He went on to work through every phase of the movement, strewing his pictures with unforgettable dream images. By contrast, Dadaist Kurt Schwitters' work "Dreams and Debris" changed little over the years. Schwitters' "Merz" pictures (merz is the second syllable of Kommerz, the German word for "business") were composed of materials taken from junk heaps. Schwitters said, " 'Merz' stands for freedom from all fetters,—for the sake of artistic creation." And he carried on with his Merz creations until his death in 1948. Schwitters gathered up the debris of civilization and turned it into art—a perfect Dada gesture of defiance and irony.

The contrast between Ernst and Schwitters is instructive. The Dadaists and then the Surrealists were individuals, much too liberated to be anything so formal as a school of painters. They picked and chose among the Dada and Surrealist ideas, whether psychic automatism or flights of fancy "without any check by reason, and freed from any esthetic or moral preoccupation." All the Surrealists concurred in the "omnipotence of dreams and in the detached play of thought." But they used these ideas as artists, not as devotees.

Thus we can recognize similarities among the various Surrealists and yet acknowledge their differences. For twenty years or more Surrealism was a craze. Even Picasso flirted with it. But all the artists remained individualists: Miró is not at all like Tanguy, and Dali is not at all like Magritte, and so on . . . .

André Masson, a troubled spirit who often moved away from Surrealism, and as often returned, became the supreme catalyst of the avant-garde movement. He ushered in the Spaniard Joan Miró, the Armenian Arshile Gorky, who spent his last years in America, and finally the American Jackson Pollock.

The Act Is All

Pollock came at just the right time, when the revolutionary spirit in art was flagging. For example, few of the artists who had participated in the last official Surrealist show in Paris in 1947 had expressed their protest against World War II. Their mild reactions suggested complacency or intellectual isolation. They needed a jolt, and Pollock administered it. He outraged the world by dripping and throwing paint on vast canvases. True, he followed only one of the Dada lines: automatism, and art based

Giorgio de Chirico. The Mystery and Melancholy of a Street (1914). Private collection. The Museum of Modern Art, New York. Using desolate perspectives, sinister shadows, fantasmal figures and deserted buildings, Chirico creates an atmosphere of dream and alienation.

Arshile Gorky (left). The Betrothal II (1947). Whitney Museum of American Art, New York. In this painting, done a year before Gorky's death, the forms are sensual but often pinched and nervous as though to suggest the pains of sex along with its delights.

Jean Arp (right). Yellow Constellation (1953). A founder of Dadaism and Surrealism, Jean Arp, an Alsatian, declared that he submitted his compositions to the laws of chance, but his work achieves formal rhythms that seem anything but accidental. (Sidney Janis Gallery)

Yves Tanguy (below). Time and Again . . . Never (1942). Tanguy was a French-born painter who began to paint in 1925 without previous training. His graceful amoebic forms float in the cool lights of a mist-covered sea. (Pierre Matisse Gallery)

Jean Tinguely. Homage to New York (1960).
One of the great spoofs of the "neo-Dada"
movement, this contraption, described as "self-
constructing and self-destroying," actually
destroyed itself during a demonstration, with
the Swiss-born Tinguely at the "controls."

Salvador Dali. Rainy Taxi (1938).
Original at Exposition Internationale du
Surréalisme, Paris.
This nightmarish mockery of a taxicab, sprout-
ing weird vegetation and occupied by two horrid
figures, is the three-dimensional embodiment
of a sick dream, at once revolting and funny.

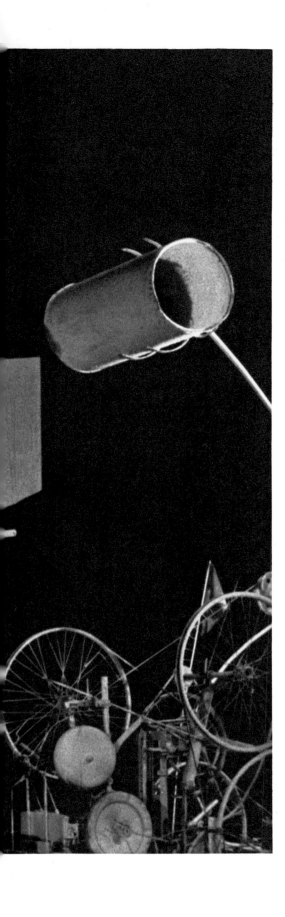

largely on chance. His contribution was to shift the emphasis away from the finished, polished paintings of the Surrealists, and put it back on the act of creation, the action of painting.

A hard look still finds reflections of Dada in many studios and galleries, wherever art has broken with traditional definitions of art, or wherever there is rage at conventions that do not answer the needs of modern life. Its spirit infuses most of the art that has surprised, puzzled or outraged us in recent years, whether it is Pop art, which is a light-hearted but serious-minded scrutiny of everyday objects, or junk art that welds debris into ironic tributes to mechanization, or Op art that dizzies the viewer—deliberately. It reigns in Happenings where anything can happen, and nothing is controlled by any tradition or rule. It is most true to its own spirit when it refuses to be captured, defined, given a name or hung in a museum. Jean Tingueley's monumental junk construction entitled "Homage to New York" was its epitome. At its unveiling in 1960 it huffed and creaked and in a few minutes destroyed itself.

Masters of Protest

by Dick Brukenfeld

Chiefs of government and other members of the establishment come and go, but corruption, injustice, poverty and war abide forever—or at least for the forseeable future. The failings of social and political institutions and the flaws of individual men have, since the Renaissance, provided subject matter for artists who wanted to probe and protest the human condition.

To be moved by their works we need not know the specific conditions which prompted them, because such conditions have been with us since the Serpent sold a bill of goods to Adam and Eve. It makes little difference today, for example, whether Bruegel's "Blind Leading the Blind" was directed against slavish following of the established church or slavish following of the reform movement. We are not strangers to the image of men being led blindly to the brink.

Caricature, Romanticism, Expressionism, Dada, and Social Realism are the labels scholars have pinned on the art of social comment. Yet the works that continue to interest us are those of individual men who have pressed beyond the strictures of any ism in art or politics. Even in modern Mexican painting, so closely linked to the revolutionary movement, José Clemente Orozco and David Alfaro Siqueiros have made the mural a medium for their personal views. Siqueiros, often in the headlines and once imprisoned for his left-wing activities, can be accused only of humanism and individualism in his "Our Present Image." With grace and strength he gives us his singular interpretation of a condition universal today—the reaching out for an identity.

When an artist subordinates his individuality to become a tool of a group, the result is not social comment but social propaganda. It is no wonder that Soviet art looks the same today as it did in the 1930's. Still harnessed to the role of pamphleteer, the Soviet artist continues to paint the same advertisements for the party, the worker, the state. Similarly, the more doctrinaire

products of American art in the 1930's have little continuing interest. By contrast, such paintings of that period as Ben Shahn's Sacco and Vanzetti series, which penetrate rather than preach, have lost none of their impact.

Although the artist of social comment is a skeptical, anti-establishment individualist, he is traditional in painting the appearance of things. He does not, however, reproduce reality; he dramatizes his reactions to conditions and events. He seeks out the drama in suffering and conflict, and drives home the contrast between what men aspire to and what they achieve. The commentator is also traditional in being a member of the loyal opposition. No matter how critical he feels about his society, he is still part of it. That society buys his works, allows his dissent, supplies a certain security, and, most important, provides a target. Without an establishment, there can be no anti-establishment. The artist of social comment plays the devil's advocate in the dialogue which all so-called free societies allow.

It is no accident that the art which probes and protests man's condition—like the free society itself—developed during the Renaissance. The challenge to established authority and the assertion that man has the ability to judge for himself is an essence of that age. Few works of art better express that challenge than Bruegel's "Blind Leading the Blind." Visualized here is the disaster that results when men surrender their individual perception to gain the security of the "organization."

But the main body of artistic comment on the effects of the Renaissance appeared during the eighteenth and nineteenth centuries. Beginning with William Hogarth's scenes from contemporary English life in 1730, this first wave included Thomas Rowlandson and James Gillray, English humorous commentators, continued through Francisco Goya under the monarchy in Spain, and ended in France with the death of Honoré Daumier in 1879.

Pieter Bruegel (above). Blind Leading the Blind, 1567.
Painted, when the Reformation was well under way, this vivid interpretation of the Biblical parable was probably aimed at the established clergy. (Alinari-Art Reference Bureau)

William Hogarth (below). The Rake's Progress: He Revels, No. 3, 1735.
One of a series of satires that point a moral with candid scenes of vice and dissipation. (The Metropolitan Museum of Art, New York)

While they challenged the establishment, these painters were also making a stir in the world of art. Instead of re-interpreting scenes from the Bible, history or mythology, they responded to life around them. They made the common man a prime subject, and they looked at him one by one. They did not distort a subject's features to conform with an established standard of beauty. On the contrary, they distorted away from the ideal, emphasizing those features which expressed individual character. When this delight in the individual was exaggerated into a kind of super-individualism, the result was caricature. Thomas Rowlandson's "Amputation" is a masterly example of caricature used to satirize the medical establishment.

Rowlandson, Gillray, Hogarth and Goya reached their largest audiences with prints that were sold singly or in series. During the nineteenth century a new medium for the artist of social comment, the journal of political opinion, appeared. "La Caricature," the first of these, then "Charivari," a daily, published Daumier's penetrating scenes of Parisian life from the July Revolution of 1830 to the Franco-Prussian War of 1870.

A second wave of social comment art came as an aftermath of the carnage of World War I. As the times moved further out of joint, artists increasingly distorted their representations of the visual world. Next to their works, the exaggerations of eighteenth and nineteenth century caricature look mild. In Pablo Picasso's "Guernica," the artist presents a whole repertoire of private symbolism and distortions. While George Grosz, Otto Dix, Max Beckmann and others underscored the beast in man and foreshadowed the coming storm, the Dada movement launched a protest against all established values and systems. Quickly developing into Surrealism, Dada seems in retrospect more significant as an artistic than a social protest.

In the Americas, new waves of social protest painting were rising both north and south of the border. The Renaissance came late and suddenly to Mexico with the Revolution of 1910–20, giving freedom and purpose to a group of muralists who believed, like Diego Rivera, that "whatever is not five times useful is not beautiful." One use for the new painting was to display the glorious past of this ancient civilization: thus the heavy, rhythmic native forms which typify modern Mexican art. Although it speaks for a group, this art expresses the personal vision of a Siqueiros or an Orozco.

In the years before World War I in the United States, Robert Henri and the realism of his so-called "ash-can school" cleared the way for the art of social comment. Seeking to create an art that was "American," an art of the common people, Henri and his followers looked for inspiration to such French painters as Courbet, Daumier and Millet, and to the naturalism of Emile Zola's novels. Descriptive rather than dramatic, the "ash-can" group expanded the vocabulary of American art to include life in the city streets. But it was the economic collapse of 1929 that ignited the flame of American protest. Responding to the effects of the Great Depression on the common man, the Social Realists painted much that was obvious and predictable. But three men whose attack is distinctly personal still speak to us with vigor and meaning—Ben Shahn, Philip Evergood, and Jack Levine.

Ben Shahn reached a much wider audience than the others. With a compassionate brush he recorded his view of incidents progressing from the labor unrest of the 1920's to the "Voyage of the Lucky Dragon," which refers to the unlucky Japanese fishing boat that strayed too close to U.S. H-bomb tests in the Pacific. Like Shahn, Philip Evergood seeks to penetrate the universal aspects of a situation. But Evergood's vision is more surrealistic; both characters and objects radiate a restless, primitive energy. More caustic than either Shahn or Evergood, Jack Levine unmasks the establishment to expose the pockmarks on its soul. His attacks are all the more effective for being painted in the manner of the old masters.

The cutting edge of social comment is not popular in the current art scene. Americans have preferred, during the last few years, a kind of pseudo-attack that actually celebrates its target. A few contemporaries, however, are bombarding the glass houses of the establishment with real stones. David Levine's caricatures of the powerful reveal a unique ability to explore human character. Where Levine represents specific individuals, Tomi Ungerer gives us characters that are a striking and fanciful embodiment of ideas.

Because of associations with the post-World War I Dada movement, much contemporary art has been labeled neo-Dada. But the majority of today's detached and whimsical treatments of mass-produced objects are not intended as social comment. While the Dadaists, in making an art of machine-like objects, showed their rejection of "rational" man and his institutions, Pop artists use mass media and machines as subjects because they accept mass media and machines. Where Dada was pessimistic, Pop is optimistic. Dada's contribution to Pop and other contemporary styles is in the introduction of new subject matter, new materials, "ready-mades," "found" objects, and in an amusing anti-art attitude. The jet fighter and other objects in James Rosenquist's mural "F-111" have a high potential as social comment. Yet Rosenquist has succeeded in neutralizing his subject matter, avoiding provocative connotations and emotional impact.

Some critics argue that the very impersonality of the new art will make the viewer more aware of his dehumanized environment. But in practice these surface treatments have tended to glorify facades rather than expose them. Because Andy Warhol elevated Campbell Soup cans to the realm of "art," the red and white design soon decorated such objects as waste baskets, cocktail glasses and piggy banks.

Perhaps so few artists today are probing or protesting the human condition because the major waves of social comment in art have arisen when nations were in a revolution or depression, or in the aftermath of war on their own territory.

An even broader reason for the scarcity of such art is the tendency of recent art away from the representation of visual reality in the old sense. Since, moreover, the mass media show us world events so vividly and sometimes so frighteningly, many artists feel that comment is superfluous.

Pop artists go even further, believing that this sensory bombardment by the mass media has diminished man's ability to respond. Thus they offer us "hard-edged" works that are easily grasped and often toylike, and that sometimes have the appeal of a game. Yet the reaction to wars in Vietnam and in other underdeveloped nations, to revolts on our campuses and in our inner cities shows that many people are responding to what the mass media bring into their living rooms. This renaissance of awareness and commitment may well give rise to a new wave of social comment in art.

Thomas Rowlandson. Amputation, 1785. This caricature, with its sharp contrast between the business-like attitude of the doctors and the agony of the patient, still has all of its original point. (The Metropolitan Museum of Art, New York)

Francisco de Goya (left). The Disasters of War. Por qué?
One of a series of stark, nightmarish etchings made during the French invasion of Spain in 1808. (National Gallery of Art, Washington)

Honoré Daumier (below). Le Ventre Legislatif, 1834.
One of Daumier's vitriolic caricatures of the French political scene in the 1830's. (Arts Graphiques de la Cité, Paris)

George Grosz (right). Metropolis, 1917. A montage of life in Germany during World War I that captures the feverish pace of dissipation in a collapsing world. (The Museum of Modern Art, New York)

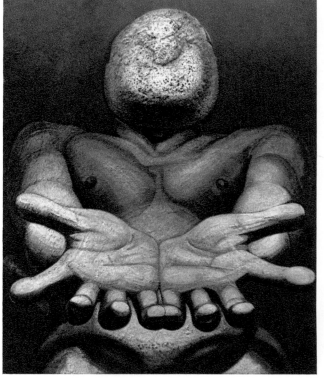

David Siqueiros. Our Present Image, 1947.
Part of a mural by the radical Mexican artist, this figure with face hidden seems to be literally reaching out for an identity. (Instituto Nacional de Bellas Artes, Mexico)

Pablo Picasso (above). Guernica, 1937. Commemorating the destruction of a Spanish town in the first planned bombing of civilians, the artist assaults us with harsh angles and lights exploding out of darkness. (On loan to the Museum of Modern Art, New York, from the artist)

José Clemente Orozco (right). Dying Indian. A fierce protester against the oppression of the Mexican Indian, Orozco painted many agonizing outbursts such as this. (Museo J. C. Orozco, Mexico)

James Rosenquist. F-111, 1965.
Instead of caricaturing controversial aspects
of contemporary American life, the artist in this
gigantic mural juxtaposes them shockingly—
as in the atomic cloud contained by colorful
umbrellas—and presents everything in a Pop
art version of popular commercial illustration.
(Leo Castelli Gallery)

George Segal. The Execution, 1967.
The artist's anonymous puppet-like plaster
figures serve well for this epitome of the
impersonal cruelty of war. (Sidney Janis
Gallery)

A poster by Raymond Savignac (facing page,
above) satirizes the Russian invasion of
Czechoslovakia, while two posters (below) by
French students rap De Gaulle's regimenta-
tion of the French people and picture him as
a huge gendarme forcibly silencing criticism.

The Inspired Line: Steinberg

by Manuel Gasser

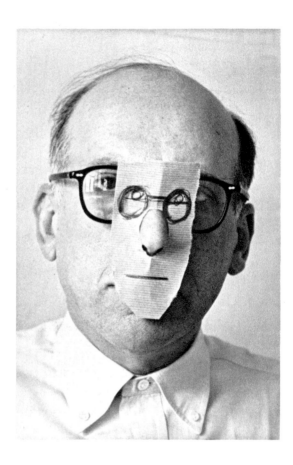

Saul Steinberg is a highly intelligent man. He is a man with the insight of a psychologist, the judgment of an art critic, the wisdom of a social philosopher. If he wrote books, he would be an expert in each of these fields. But Steinberg does not write books. He draws.

He draws analyses and diagnoses, aphorisms and statements. And his drawings are more sharply observed, more effectively composed, and more forcefully formulated than most things written nowadays on the world situation and man's frame of mind. Although he means his work seriously, he presents it in a way that at first appears harmless, playful and most amusing. Only when we look more closely at his "caricatures" and "cartoons" do we realize that there is more behind them than wit, abundance of ideas and an amazing drawing talent.

His New York street scene, for instance, turns out to be a veritable vision of hell: poisonous vapors emerge from sewer covers, a hotel extends an awning like a suction pipe, witches ride the taxis, and a woman leads a wild beast on a leash. The policeman's steed is half horse and half wolf, and he himself is an incarnation of evil power. In the background babylon-like towers with polyp-like balconies rise into nothingness. And the Chrysler building presents itself as half "juke-box" and half Indian totem pole.

Here is criticism that expresses a chilling fear of the blessings of the Brave New World and shows everyday objects converted into hallucinations and fantasies.

He goes a step further in the drawing that shows six or seven visitors to an art gallery. Only one of them is human, three are completely deformed, one appears to be a birdman, and the other two are reduced to the letter D and a question mark. At first glance, this seems to be little more than a graphic joke based on a familiar scene. But we find ourselves not quite satisfied with this explanation. We start wondering, searching for further hidden meanings. And suddenly we realize that in this drawing two psychological mechanisms of art viewers are vividly exposed. One is the fact that everyone responds differently—and sometimes queerly—to one and the same picture, and the other is that a work of art has the power to change the observer insofar as it increases or exaggerates his peculiar character. In other words this is an x-ray picture of the art consumer.

We must solve a puzzle in every work of Steinberg's. Sometimes the solution is easy, as in the drawing that shows endless ranks of marching and posing figures: this demonstrates the uniformity of modern life more impressively than any learned treatise on mass society. In other examples, as in that of the Indians pursuing the bicyclists, several interpretations are possible. In some cases, such as the three sirens under the full moon, the picture remains a dream full of hybrid monsters.

Always, however, Steinberg achieves his goal: to shake the observer out of his lethargy and to challenge him until he decides to think and judge independently.

STEINBERG
1966

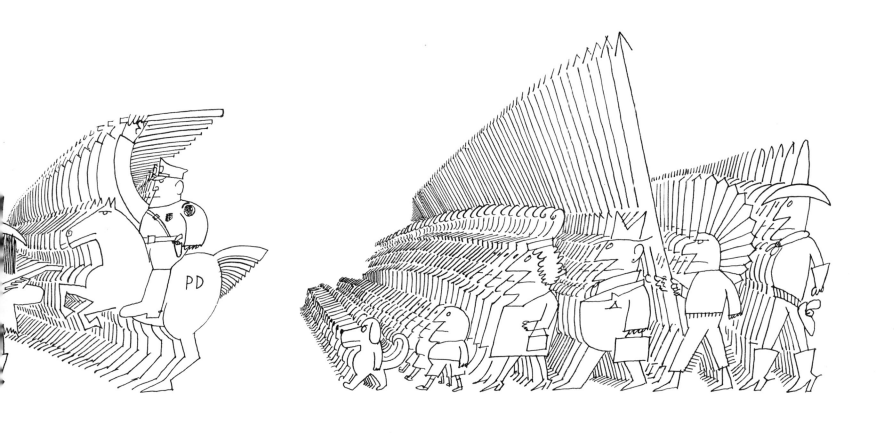

Notes on Contributors

in the order of their contributions

Charlotte Willard is an art critic who appears in Look magazine and Art in America and was until recently art editor of the New York Post.

Elenore Lester is a critic of art and drama whose articles have appeared in the New York Times Magazine and whose book on the arts will be published shortly by MacMillan.

Allen Hurlburt, now Director of Design for Cowles Communications Inc., was for many years Art Director of Look magazine.

Shareen Blair, a specialist in fine arts picture research, was formerly a leading dancer with the Merce Cunningham company.

Nancy Kaufman was on the staff of American Heritage Publishing Co. for five years and is now a free-lance writer and researcher in art.

Owen Rachleff was a staff writer for an art book publisher and is the author of Rembrandt's Life of Christ, Great Bible Stories and Master Paintings, and articles on art for Horizon and other periodicals. He also gives a course in the sources of art at the New School.

Wallace Brockway, a consulting editor for the Bollingen Foundation, is author of The Albert Lasker Collection: Renoir to Matisse, Men of Music, and other books on the arts.

Dick Brukenfeld is a writer for the major radio and television networks. One of his special interests is modern art.

Manuel Gasser has for many years been the editor of Du, the distinguished Swiss magazine of art and culture. He has written about Steinberg in Du.

Index